Eternal Embrace
A Journey Through Valentine Week

Introduction

Love is a force that has shaped human history, inspired countless works of art, and defined relationships in profound ways. It is more than just an emotion; it is an experience, a journey that evolves and deepens over time. Among the many celebrations of love, Valentine's Week stands out as a unique and cherished tradition that encapsulates romance, commitment, and companionship. Spanning seven days, each dedicated to a different expression of love—from the innocence of gifting a rose to the depth of a heartfelt promise—this week allows lovers to celebrate their bond in meaningful ways. But beyond the chocolates, gifts, and grand gestures, lies the essence of true love: connection, understanding, and an eternal embrace that transcends time.

Valentine's Week is not just about romantic relationships; it is about celebrating love in all its forms. Whether it is the love between friends, family members, or even self-love, this week serves as a reminder that affection and appreciation should be nurtured in every aspect of life. In a world that often moves too fast, where daily routines overshadow emotions, Valentine's Week offers an opportunity to pause, reflect, and express gratitude for those who make life more beautiful. Each day leading up to Valentine's Day holds significance, symbolizing different facets of love—from the excitement of new beginnings to the warmth of unwavering companionship. It is a time to cherish past memories, create new ones, and reaffirm the importance of love in our lives.

As we embark on this journey through Valentine's Week, Eternal Embrace invites you to explore the deeper meanings behind these seven days. This book is not just about traditions or rituals; it is about understanding the emotions that fuel these celebrations. With each chapter, we will delve into the significance of love, the power of small gestures, and the timeless beauty of romance. Whether you are experiencing love for the first time or rekindling an old flame, this journey will inspire you to embrace love wholeheartedly—not just for a week, but for a lifetime.

Chapter 1
Rose Day – The Bloom of Affection

Roses have long been a symbol of love, passion, and admiration, making them the perfect emblem to begin the journey of Valentine's Week. Rose Day, celebrated on February 7th, marks the first step in expressing emotions that words often fail to capture. The simple act of gifting a rose holds deep meaning—it signifies appreciation, affection, and sometimes even a silent confession of love. Across cultures and generations, roses have been used to communicate unspoken feelings, bridging hearts with their beauty and fragrance. Whether it is a deep red rose symbolizing true love, a pink one representing admiration, or a yellow rose reflecting friendship, each bloom carries a message that can touch the soul in profound ways.

Beyond its aesthetic charm, the rose has a poetic essence that resonates with the emotions of the heart. It reminds us that love, like a rose, is delicate yet powerful, capable of bringing immense joy yet requiring care and nurturing. Just as a rosebud slowly unfolds its petals, love too blossoms over time, revealing its depth layer by layer. The act of giving a rose on this day is not just a gesture but a promise—one that signifies the beginning of something special, a bond that will grow stronger with time. Whether exchanged between new lovers, longtime partners, or even between friends, the gift of a rose conveys warmth, respect, and an appreciation for the beauty of connection.

As we celebrate Rose Day, it is important to look beyond the flower itself and embrace the emotions it represents. Love is not measured by extravagant gestures but by the sincerity behind them. A single rose, given with genuine affection, can speak louder than a thousand words. It serves as a reminder to cherish the love we have, to express gratitude for those who bring joy into our lives, and to nurture relationships with the same care we would give to a delicate bloom. The bloom of affection begins here, setting the stage for the heartfelt journey through Valentine's Week.

The Language of Roses

For centuries, roses have been more than just flowers; they have been symbols of deep emotions, each color conveying a unique message. The tradition of using roses to express feelings dates back to ancient civilizations, where flowers were often exchanged as silent messengers of love, admiration, and even sorrow. The Victorians took this floral communication to new heights, developing an entire language known as floriography, where every flower, and even the way it was presented, carried a specific meaning. Today, roses remain one of the most powerful expressions of human emotions, with each hue whispering a different sentiment to the recipient.

A red rose is the ultimate symbol of deep love and passion. It embodies the essence of romance, making it the most commonly gifted flower on Rose Day and Valentine's Day. The intensity of red reflects the strength of emotions—be it love, desire, or commitment. A bouquet of red roses can signify a profound declaration of love, while a single red rose often represents a heartfelt confession. Darker shades of red symbolize deep devotion and respect, while a bright, fiery red can represent new and exciting love. Those who choose to give red roses are often expressing emotions that go beyond words, letting the beauty of the flower articulate their affection.

On the other hand, a pink rose exudes elegance, admiration, and gratitude. It is often associated with gentle emotions such as appreciation, joy, and sweet affection. Lighter shades of pink convey innocence and happiness, making them ideal for expressing budding love or admiration. Deeper pink hues symbolize gratitude and recognition, often given as a token of appreciation to friends, mentors, or loved ones. Unlike the passionate energy of red roses, pink roses have a softer, more nurturing essence, making them perfect for relationships built on mutual respect and care.

A yellow rose carries a completely different message—one of friendship, warmth, and happiness. Unlike red roses, which are tied to romance, yellow roses are a celebration of companionship and joy. They radiate positivity and are often given to brighten someone's day or to reaffirm the bond of a deep friendship. In the past, yellow roses were sometimes associated with jealousy, but today, they are widely recognized as a symbol of platonic love and cheerfulness. They are the perfect choice for celebrating a meaningful friendship or for expressing gratitude toward someone who brings sunshine into your life.

A white rose, with its pristine beauty, represents purity, innocence, and new beginnings. It is often used in weddings, symbolizing the purity of love and the start of a new journey together. White roses can also express reverence, making them a common choice for honoring someone's memory. When given in romantic settings, they signify the promise of a fresh and sincere love, untainted by past experiences. They are the flowers of new possibilities and quiet devotion, ideal for those who believe in the power of pure, unconditional love.

Other roses, such as orange roses, symbolize enthusiasm and desire, bridging the gap between friendship and passionate love. They are vibrant and energetic, often given when admiration turns into deeper affection. Lavender roses are rare and unique, symbolizing enchantment and love at first sight, while blue roses, though artificially created, represent mystery and the unattainable. Black roses, often misunderstood, signify endings, but they can also represent rebirth, transformation, or deep, undying devotion.

Understanding the language of roses allows us to communicate emotions in a way that transcends words. Whether given to a lover, a friend, or a family member, each rose carries an unspoken message that speaks directly to the heart. Choosing the right color adds depth to our expressions, making the act of gifting a rose not just a gesture, but a meaningful symbol of the emotions we hold dear.

Gifting Flowers with Meaning

Flowers have long been a medium for expressing emotions, and among them, roses hold a special place in the language of love. Often called the "queen of flowers," roses are more than just beautiful blooms; they are messengers of deep sentiments, carrying hidden meanings based on their color, number, and even the way they are presented. This unspoken language of roses has been cherished across cultures for centuries, allowing lovers, friends, and admirers to convey feelings that words may struggle to express. From the passionate red rose to the delicate white bloom of innocence, every shade has a story to tell.

The Meaning Behind Rose Colors

One of the most fascinating aspects of the language of roses is the significance of their colors. The classic red rose is universally recognized as a symbol of deep love and desire. It represents passionate romance, making it the most popular choice for Valentine's Day and romantic declarations. A bouquet of red roses is often a grand gesture of love, a way of saying "I love you" without uttering a single word. On the other hand, pink roses convey admiration, gratitude, and appreciation. They are often gifted to express feelings of tenderness and gentle affection, making them a perfect choice for new relationships or close friendships.

White roses signify purity, innocence, and new beginnings. They are often seen at weddings, symbolizing a fresh start filled with sincerity and devotion. In contrast, yellow roses embody friendship, joy, and warmth. Unlike other romantic shades, yellow roses are a cheerful way to show appreciation for a close friend or someone who brings happiness into one's life. Meanwhile, orange roses represent enthusiasm, excitement, and fascination, often given when someone wants to express admiration in a more energetic and vibrant way. Finally, lavender roses symbolize enchantment and love at first sight, making them an intriguing choice for someone who wants to express a sense of wonder and admiration.

The Significance of Numbers and Presentation

Beyond color, the number of roses in a bouquet also carries a special meaning. A single rose is often a simple yet profound way to say, "You are my one and only." A dozen roses symbolize complete and perfect love, while two roses intertwined signify a shared connection and deep bond between two individuals. Giving three roses conveys the heartfelt message of "I love you," and six roses indicate a desire to be loved in return. If someone gifts eleven roses, it means, "You are my treasured one," while a full hundred roses is the ultimate declaration of undying love and devotion.

Even the way a rose is presented plays a role in its message. A rose given with its stem pointing downwards might indicate rejection, whereas a fully bloomed rose with buds signifies an evolving love, growing stronger over time. Similarly, gifting a rose without thorns symbolizes love at first sight, free from obstacles or hesitation.

In essence, roses are more than just flowers—they are a powerful expression of emotions, a timeless way to communicate love, appreciation, and devotion. Whether gifted in romance, friendship, or admiration, each rose carries a message that can touch hearts and strengthen connections, making them an enduring symbol in the journey of love.

A Journey Through Romance

Romance is more than just grand gestures, poetic words, or fleeting moments of passion—it is a journey that unfolds over time, shaped by shared experiences, emotions, and an unspoken understanding between two souls. It is a path paved with tenderness, excitement, and at times, challenges that test the strength of love. The essence of romance lies not only in the magical beginnings but in the way it evolves, deepens, and transforms as two people navigate life together. From the spark of first attraction to the comfort of unwavering companionship, romance is a dance of emotions, where every step taken is a testament to the connection between two hearts.

Every love story begins with a moment—an encounter, a glance, a conversation that sets everything into motion. The early stages of romance are filled with excitement, curiosity, and discovery. It is a time when lovers explore each other's worlds, finding joy in the smallest details and cherishing every stolen glance or whispered word. There is an undeniable thrill in the unknown, in the anticipation of what is yet to come. The first dates, the long conversations, the exchange of meaningful gifts—each moment is a building block that shapes the foundation of a relationship. It is in this stage that romance feels like a dream, where time seems to pause, and the world revolves around the presence of that one special person.

Yet, as love matures, romance takes on a deeper and more meaningful form. It is no longer just about the rush of emotions but about the comfort of knowing that someone truly understands and accepts you. Romance is found in the quiet moments—a reassuring touch, a shared silence, or the warmth of waking up next to someone who feels like home. It is in the small, thoughtful gestures that show love without the need for words. Bringing someone their favorite coffee, remembering the little things that make them smile, or simply being there through life's ups and downs—these are the moments that define true romance. It is about standing together through storms, growing together through challenges, and finding joy in the ordinary.

But romance is not without its trials. Love is a journey that demands patience, understanding, and effort. There are times when misunderstandings arise, when distance creeps in, or when life's struggles test the depth of a bond. Yet, it is in these moments that the true strength of romance is revealed. A love that is nurtured, cared for, and prioritized will weather any storm. Romance is not about perfection; it is about choosing each other every single day, despite imperfections and hardships. It is about holding on when times are tough and celebrating when times are beautiful.

As we journey through romance, we come to realize that love is not just a feeling—it is a commitment, a shared experience, a story that is written in countless moments, big and small. Romance is not just about the beginning; it is about the way love endures, grows, and becomes an eternal embrace that stands the test of time.

Chapter 2
Propose Day – The Art of Confession

Love, at its core, is a beautiful emotion, but expressing it takes courage, sincerity, and vulnerability. Propose Day, celebrated on February 8th, is dedicated to those who wish to confess their deepest feelings and take the next step in their romantic journey. It is a day filled with anticipation, excitement, and sometimes even nervousness, as people gather the strength to voice what their hearts have been longing to say. Whether it is the first confession of love, a proposal for a lifetime commitment, or a heartfelt expression of devotion, this day holds immense significance in the journey of romance. A proposal is not just about the words spoken; it is about the emotions behind them, the sincerity in one's eyes, and the unspoken promise of a future together.

The act of proposing has been a cherished tradition across cultures, with each love story unfolding in its own unique way. Some proposals are grand and extravagant, involving candlelit dinners, breathtaking landscapes, or even surprise gestures that take months of planning. Others are simple yet deeply meaningful, where a heartfelt confession in an intimate setting carries more weight than a thousand elaborate arrangements. Regardless of how it is done, a proposal marks a pivotal moment in a relationship—one that holds the power to change the course of two lives forever. It is a testament to trust, commitment, and the willingness to embrace love with an open heart.

Yet, beyond the excitement and romance, Propose Day is also a day of reflection. It is a time to understand what love truly means and whether one is ready for the responsibilities that come with it. A proposal is not just about asking a question—it is about promising a future of love, patience, and unwavering support. The beauty of this day lies in the courage it takes to express one's emotions, the vulnerability of laying one's heart bare, and the hope that love will be reciprocated with the same intensity. Whether the answer is a joyful "yes" or a thoughtful pause, every proposal is a step in the journey of love, teaching us the value of honesty, connection, and the profound power of heartfelt confession.

Overcoming the Fear of Rejection

The fear of rejection is one of the most powerful emotions that can hold a person back from expressing their true feelings. When it comes to confessing love or proposing a lifelong commitment, this fear often becomes overwhelming, making people second-guess their emotions, their words, and even their worth. The thought of hearing a "no" can be paralyzing, leading many to suppress their feelings rather than risk the pain of rejection. However, love, at its core, requires courage—courage to be vulnerable, to take a chance, and to embrace the unknown. Overcoming the fear of rejection is not just about increasing the chances of a positive response but about gaining confidence in oneself and understanding that rejection is not a reflection of one's value, but rather a part of life's journey.

One of the key ways to combat the fear of rejection is to shift perspective. Instead of seeing rejection as a failure, it should be viewed as an opportunity for growth. Every experience, whether successful or not, teaches valuable lessons about love, relationships, and personal strength. If a proposal or confession of love is met with rejection, it does not mean that the love was not real or that the person is unworthy of being loved. It simply means that the feelings were not reciprocated in the way one had hoped, and that is okay. In fact, experiencing rejection can sometimes be a blessing in disguise, steering a person toward someone who will appreciate and cherish them in the way they deserve. By reframing rejection as a stepping stone rather than an endpoint, it becomes easier to approach love with a brave and open heart.

Preparation and self-awareness also play a crucial role in overcoming this fear. Before making a proposal or confessing love, it is important to understand one's own emotions and the depth of connection shared with the other person. Building a strong foundation of trust, communication, and mutual respect can make a proposal feel less like a leap into the unknown and more like a natural progression of the relationship. Additionally, practicing confidence, whether through self-affirmation, visualization, or even rehearsing what to say, can help ease nerves. The key is to express love with sincerity and without attachment to the outcome. Love should not be conditional upon acceptance; rather, it should be about expressing genuine emotions, regardless of the response.

At its core, the fear of rejection is rooted in the fear of losing something valuable—be it love, dignity, or self-esteem. However, true love is not just about receiving love in return; it is about having the courage to express it openly and freely. Whether the response is a "yes" or a "no," the act of confessing love is, in itself, a beautiful and courageous step. It signifies personal growth, emotional maturity, and the willingness to embrace love wholeheartedly. In the end, rejection is not what defines a person—it is the way they rise from it, learn from it, and continue to believe in the magic of love that truly matters.

Crafting the Perfect Proposal

A proposal is one of the most memorable moments in a love story—a moment filled with emotion, anticipation, and the promise of a future together. While grand gestures and elaborate surprises can make a proposal spectacular, the true essence of a perfect proposal lies in its sincerity and personal touch. It is not about impressing the world; it is about creating a heartfelt experience that resonates deeply with the person receiving it. Every love story is unique, and so should be the proposal. Whether it is a simple, intimate moment or an extravagant, cinematic event, the key to crafting the perfect proposal is understanding the emotions, values, and shared experiences that define the relationship.

The first step in planning the perfect proposal is to consider the personality and preferences of the person being proposed to. Some people dream of a public, grand declaration of love, while others prefer something private and intimate. Understanding what makes them feel special ensures that the proposal aligns with their comfort and happiness. A romantic dinner under the stars, a handwritten letter expressing the depth of one's love, or even a spontaneous proposal in a meaningful location can be far more touching than a highly publicized event. The setting should hold significance—perhaps the place where the couple first met, where they shared a memorable date, or a destination they both love. Thoughtfulness in choosing the right location enhances the emotional impact of the moment.

Another crucial element is personalization. A proposal should reflect the unique journey of the relationship. Incorporating shared memories, inside jokes, or sentimental elements can make the proposal feel even more meaningful. For instance, referencing an old conversation about dream proposals, playing a song that holds significance, or even including family or friends (if it aligns with the couple's dynamic) can make the moment unforgettable. The way the question is asked also matters—speaking from the heart, being authentic, and expressing genuine emotions create a proposal that feels natural and profound. While some may prepare a detailed speech, others may simply let the moment flow naturally. The most important thing is that the words come from a place of deep love and truth.

Beyond the moment itself, planning the details can add to the magic of the proposal. Choosing the right ring (or a symbol of commitment) that resonates with the partner's taste, planning a post-proposal celebration, and even thinking about capturing the moment—whether through photographs or by creating a quiet, cherished memory—enhances the experience. However, while preparation is important, leaving room for spontaneity and genuine emotion is equally essential. The perfect proposal is not about perfection in execution; it is about the depth of feeling behind it.

At its core, a proposal is not just about asking a question; it is about expressing a desire to build a future together. Whether elaborate or simple, planned for months or done in a moment of pure emotion, the perfect proposal is one that is filled with love, sincerity, and the beautiful promise of forever.

When Love Finds Its Voice

Love is one of the most profound and beautiful emotions a person can experience, yet it is also one of the hardest to express. Often, people feel the intensity of love within their hearts but struggle to put it into words, fearing rejection, misunderstanding, or the inability to fully convey the depth of their emotions. However, there comes a moment when love finds its voice—a moment when emotions overflow, and words, no matter how imperfect, become the bridge that connects two souls. This is the essence of a confession of love or a heartfelt proposal. When love finally speaks, it brings clarity, courage, and the power to change lives forever.

The journey of love is often filled with silent admiration, unspoken emotions, and moments of hesitation. People hesitate to confess their feelings due to self-doubt, fear of rejection, or the uncertainty of how the other person will respond. Yet, holding back love only creates longing and regret. When love finds its voice, it liberates the heart from its own fears, allowing the truth to be spoken with sincerity. A simple yet genuine "I love you" has the power to transform relationships, deepen bonds, and open the doors to new beginnings. It is not about perfect timing, grand gestures, or poetic words—it is about honesty, vulnerability, and the courage to share what the heart truly feels.

Expressing love is not just about verbal confessions; it is about the emotions behind the words. Love speaks through actions, gestures, and the way two people care for each other. A tender gaze, a reassuring touch, a heartfelt letter, or even the smallest acts of kindness can express love more powerfully than words alone. When love finds its voice, it is not just about saying "I love you"—it is about showing it in ways that make the other person feel cherished, valued, and understood. Love is a language that goes beyond spoken words; it is a presence, a feeling, a connection that is felt in the way two hearts resonate with each other.

The moment of confession, whether through a proposal or a heartfelt admission, marks a turning point in any relationship. It is a step toward authenticity, a declaration of commitment, and an invitation to embark on a shared journey. When love is finally voiced, it creates an unbreakable bond, built on trust and emotional honesty. Even if the response is not what one hopes for, the act of expressing love itself is powerful—it signifies growth, courage, and the willingness to embrace life with an open heart. True love does not fear vulnerability; it thrives on it.

In the end, love is meant to be shared, not hidden. When love finds its voice, it becomes a force that transcends fear, hesitation, and uncertainty. It is in these moments—when love is spoken with truth and sincerity—that the heart experiences its most beautiful freedom. Whether reciprocated or not, love, when expressed, has already fulfilled its purpose: to bring light, warmth, and meaning to the journey of life.

Chapter 3
Chocolate Day – Sweetening the Bond

Love, much like chocolate, is a delightful experience that engages the senses, bringing warmth, comfort, and joy. Chocolate Day, celebrated on February 9th, is a time-honored tradition that symbolizes the sweetness and richness of love. Just as chocolate melts in the mouth and fills the heart with happiness, love too has the power to dissolve worries and deepen connections. This day is not just about exchanging chocolates but about celebrating the little moments of togetherness, indulgence, and affection that make relationships special. Whether given as a token of new love, a gesture of appreciation, or a reaffirmation of long-standing commitment, chocolate has a way of bringing people closer, making Chocolate Day a cherished part of Valentine's Week.

The tradition of gifting chocolate dates back centuries, rooted in the belief that chocolate is more than just a treat—it is a symbol of desire, passion, and emotional connection. Ancient civilizations, such as the Aztecs and Mayans, considered cocoa a divine gift, often using it in ceremonies and as a token of love. Today, the act of sharing chocolate represents warmth, care, and the willingness to add sweetness to someone's life. Each type of chocolate carries its own meaning: dark chocolate signifies deep, intense love; milk chocolate represents comfort and affection; white chocolate embodies purity and innocence, while assorted chocolates symbolize excitement and adventure in a relationship. Regardless of the type, the message remains the same—love is meant to be savored and enjoyed.

Beyond its symbolic meaning, Chocolate Day is a reminder that relationships, like chocolate, require a balance of sweetness and depth. Just as chocolate is crafted with precision, blending the right ingredients to create a perfect taste, love too requires patience, effort, and a mix of emotions to grow stronger. It is not just about grand gestures but about the small, meaningful acts of kindness that build a lasting bond. Whether it is sharing a box of chocolates, reminiscing over sweet memories, or simply indulging in the joy of each other's presence, this day reinforces the idea that love, when nurtured with care, only becomes more fulfilling over time.

The History of Love and Chocolate

The connection between love and chocolate dates back centuries, intertwining rich traditions, ancient beliefs, and evolving customs that have turned chocolate into a universal symbol of romance. The sweet indulgence that we now associate with Valentine's Day and affectionate gestures was once considered a sacred gift, reserved for royalty, rituals, and passionate expressions of devotion. From the ancient civilizations of the Mayans and Aztecs to the European courts of the Renaissance, chocolate has been cherished not only for its delicious taste but also for its mystical ability to ignite emotions, enhance desire, and strengthen bonds between lovers.

The origins of chocolate as a symbol of love can be traced to the ancient Mayan and Aztec civilizations, where cacao was considered a divine offering from the gods. The Mayans revered cacao as "the food of the gods" and often used it in sacred ceremonies, including wedding rituals. Drinking a bitter cacao brew, known as xocoatl, was believed to provide strength and vitality, making it an essential part of marriage celebrations. Similarly, the Aztecs saw cacao as a powerful aphrodisiac. Emperor Montezuma II, famous for his lavish lifestyle, was said to consume vast amounts of chocolate to enhance his energy and passion. Cacao beans were so highly valued in these civilizations that they were even used as currency, emphasizing their importance not only as a luxury but also as a treasured commodity linked to love and prosperity.

When chocolate arrived in Europe during the 16th century, it quickly became associated with romance and luxury. Spanish explorers, including Hernán Cortés, brought cacao from the New World to the European aristocracy, where it was sweetened with sugar and spices to appeal to European tastes. Soon, chocolate became a favored delicacy in royal courts, especially in France and Italy, where it was believed to have enchanting and amorous properties. The association between chocolate and love flourished as European nobles exchanged chocolates as tokens of affection, and by the 18th century, the act of gifting chocolate had become a romantic tradition. It was during this period that chocolate began to take on its modern form, with the invention of chocolate bars, truffles, and confectionery that further solidified its role in love and courtship.

The modern tradition of chocolate and love was cemented in the 19th century when British chocolatier Richard Cadbury introduced the first heart-shaped box of chocolates for Valentine's Day. This innovation transformed chocolate into an essential part of romantic gestures, making it a staple of courtship, anniversaries, and declarations of love. As chocolate production expanded and became more accessible, it became the perfect gift to express affection, appreciation, and passion. Today, chocolate remains one of the most popular symbols of love, whether in the form of a simple bar shared between partners or an extravagant box of assorted chocolates given on Valentine's Day.

The deep-rooted history of love and chocolate reveals that this sweet treat is far more than just a dessert—it is a timeless expression of romance, passion, and devotion. Whether gifted as a symbol of admiration or enjoyed as a shared indulgence, chocolate continues to be a cherished part of love's language, bringing people closer with every bite.

Sharing Sweet Moments

Love is often found in the little moments—the gentle laughter shared over coffee, the quiet walks hand in hand, the spontaneous gestures that make the heart feel cherished. Chocolate Day is a celebration of such moments, an opportunity to indulge in sweetness and strengthen the bonds of love. Just as chocolate melts in the mouth, filling the senses with warmth and joy, love too thrives in moments of shared happiness and affection. It is not about extravagant gifts or grand displays of passion but about the small, meaningful experiences that create lasting memories. Sharing chocolate on this day symbolizes the desire to bring joy into a loved one's life, to offer comfort, and to create moments that are as delightful as the treat itself.

One of the most beautiful aspects of Chocolate Day is its ability to bring people closer, not just romantically but in all relationships. A simple chocolate bar shared between friends can be a token of appreciation, a box of chocolates gifted to a parent can express gratitude, and a sweet treat given to a child can be a gesture of warmth and love. In romantic relationships, the act of giving chocolate goes beyond its rich taste—it becomes a moment of connection, a way to express affection without the need for words. Whether it's a carefully selected gourmet chocolate or a homemade dessert prepared with love, the thought behind the gesture matters more than the gift itself. The joy of watching a loved one smile while savoring a piece of chocolate creates a feeling of closeness that strengthens emotional bonds.

Beyond gift-giving, Chocolate Day is a reminder to slow down and enjoy life's sweet moments together. In today's fast-paced world, where schedules are packed, and distractions are endless, taking the time to sit together, share a treat, and appreciate each other's presence can be incredibly meaningful. Couples can turn this day into an intimate experience by baking together, exploring new chocolate flavors, or simply enjoying a cozy evening with hot chocolate and heartfelt conversation. These moments, however simple, create memories that linger far beyond the day itself.

Moreover, chocolate has long been associated with happiness, as it stimulates the release of endorphins, the body's natural "feel-good" chemicals. This scientific connection between chocolate and joy further reinforces its role in love and relationships. When shared, chocolate becomes more than just a dessert—it becomes a catalyst for bonding, laughter, and emotional warmth. A small piece of chocolate offered with love has the power to transform an ordinary moment into something special, making Chocolate Day not just about indulgence but about deepening connections.

Ultimately, Chocolate Day is a celebration of love in all its forms—romantic, familial, and even self-love. It reminds us that the sweetest moments in life are often the simplest ones, shared with the people who matter most. Whether it's through a single chocolate truffle, a heartfelt note, or a shared dessert, the essence of this day lies in the joy of giving, receiving, and savoring love's sweetest expressions.

Indulgence and Connection

Love and indulgence have always been intertwined, as both bring a sense of fulfillment, joy, and warmth to the heart. Chocolate Day is not just about exchanging chocolates; it is about indulging in the sweetness of love and deepening the connection between two people. Just as chocolate is meant to be savored, relationships too require moments of indulgence—moments where partners slow down, appreciate each other, and allow themselves to enjoy the presence of love without distraction. Indulgence is often seen as a luxury, but in love, it is a necessity. It is about treating love with care, taking the time to nurture the bond, and celebrating the simple yet profound joy of togetherness.

There is something deeply intimate about sharing a piece of chocolate with a loved one. The act of giving a chocolate, watching their face light up with delight, and sharing a moment of happiness strengthens emotional ties. Chocolate, known for its ability to stimulate pleasure centers in the brain, enhances feelings of warmth, comfort, and connection. This is why couples often exchange chocolates as a token of affection—it is not just the taste but the emotion behind it that matters. Indulgence in love does not always have to be extravagant; sometimes, it is found in the smallest moments—a bite of a shared dessert, a warm embrace, or an evening spent reminiscing over past memories while enjoying a favorite chocolate treat.

Beyond romantic love, Chocolate Day also serves as a reminder to indulge in meaningful connections with family and friends. Love is not limited to one kind of relationship; it exists in the bonds we build with those around us. A simple chocolate gift to a parent, sibling, or close friend can serve as a reminder of appreciation and gratitude. It is a small yet powerful way to say, "I cherish you, and you bring sweetness into my life." Even in self-love, chocolate plays a role, as treating oneself to something delightful is an act of self-care, a way of acknowledging one's worth and taking a moment to indulge in happiness.

Indulgence, however, is not just about consuming something sweet; it is about immersing oneself in the experience of love. In relationships, indulgence means setting aside time for one another, being fully present, and making each other feel valued. Whether it is through a romantic dinner, a handwritten note, or a simple box of chocolates, the act of indulging in love reinforces the strength of the connection. It allows partners to step away from routine, forget the stresses of daily life, and simply enjoy being with each other. Love, like chocolate, should be rich, fulfilling, and meant to be enjoyed fully.

At its heart, Chocolate Day is a celebration of indulgence and connection. It reminds us that life is not just about responsibilities and obligations but also about taking time to appreciate love in its many forms. Whether it is through a shared chocolate bar or a heartfelt moment of togetherness, this day encourages us to embrace love with open arms, indulge in its beauty, and strengthen the connections that make life truly meaningful.

Chapter 4
Teddy Day – The Comfort of Presence

Love is not only about passion and excitement but also about warmth, reassurance, and the simple comfort of knowing someone is there for you. Teddy Day, celebrated on February 10th, represents this beautiful aspect of love—the ability to provide comfort, security, and unwavering presence in someone's life. A teddy bear, with its soft embrace and gentle presence, symbolizes the warmth of love, the safety of companionship, and the emotional connection that transcends words. Just as a teddy bear becomes a source of solace during lonely moments, love too is about being there for one another, offering support, understanding, and the reassurance that one is never truly alone.

The tradition of giving teddy bears on this day goes beyond the mere act of gifting; it is an expression of affection that reminds loved ones of the emotional security they share. Unlike other gifts that may lose significance over time, a teddy bear remains a cherished keepsake, a constant reminder of the love and care it represents. Many people find comfort in hugging a teddy bear, as it mimics the warmth of a real embrace, soothing stress and bringing a sense of calm. This is why teddy bears are often gifted to those who are far away or going through a difficult time—because they serve as a tangible representation of love and presence, offering comfort even in absence.

Teddy Day also highlights the importance of emotional intimacy in relationships. Just as a teddy bear offers silent companionship, true love does not always need words to be felt. Sometimes, simply being there for someone, holding their hand during tough times, or offering a reassuring hug can mean more than any spoken expression. Love is not just about grand declarations; it is also about the quiet, reassuring presence that makes life's journey more bearable. As we celebrate this day, it is a reminder that the greatest gift we can give our loved ones is the warmth of our presence, the comfort of our embrace, and the unwavering support that makes love truly special.

Why Teddy Bears Symbolize Love

Teddy bears have long been associated with love, comfort, and emotional security. Their soft, plush embrace evokes a sense of warmth and safety, making them a cherished gift among lovers, friends, and family members. Unlike other material gifts, teddy bears hold sentimental value, often becoming treasured keepsakes that remind the recipient of the giver's love and affection. But why do teddy bears, out of all possible gifts, symbolize love so deeply? The answer lies in their connection to emotional intimacy, childhood nostalgia, and the human need for comfort and reassurance.

At the heart of this symbolism is the idea that teddy bears represent unconditional love and comfort. Just like a loving partner, a teddy bear provides a sense of presence, even in times of solitude. Its soft texture and huggable form mimic the warmth of a real embrace, offering emotional support in moments of stress, sadness, or loneliness. Many people find solace in hugging a teddy bear, as it provides a sense of security much like the embrace of a loved one. This emotional connection is what makes teddy bears more than just toys—they become symbols of care, affection, and unwavering companionship.

Teddy bears also carry a deep sense of nostalgia and innocence, reminding people of the comfort and security of childhood. Many of us had a favorite stuffed animal growing up, one that we turned to for comfort during sleepless nights or difficult days. This association with childhood innocence makes teddy bears a perfect representation of pure, unconditional love. In relationships, giving a teddy bear is a way of saying, "I am here for you," just as a childhood teddy bear once provided reassurance and emotional stability. It signifies the desire to be a constant source of comfort and love in someone's life, making it a deeply meaningful gift.

Beyond personal sentiment, teddy bears have also been historically linked to affection and emotional bonding. The tradition of gifting teddy bears as a token of love became popular in the early 20th century, as people began to associate them with romantic gestures and emotional attachment. Unlike perishable gifts like flowers or chocolates, teddy bears have a lasting presence, serving as a reminder of love even when distance or time separates people. This is why they are often given on Valentine's Day, anniversaries, and special occasions—to serve as a lasting representation of the love shared between two people.

Ultimately, teddy bears symbolize love because they represent the qualities that define a strong, healthy relationship—warmth, security, and unwavering presence. Just as a teddy bear is always there to be hugged, squeezed, and held close, love should provide the same sense of comfort and reliability. In a world that often feels fast-paced and unpredictable, the simple presence of a teddy bear serves as a gentle reminder that love, in its truest form, is always there to offer warmth, reassurance, and an embrace that never fades.

The Role of Gifts in Relationships

Gifts have always played a significant role in relationships, serving as tangible expressions of love, appreciation, and thoughtfulness. While love itself is intangible, gifts provide a physical manifestation of emotions, allowing people to communicate their feelings in a meaningful way. Whether it's a small token of affection or an extravagant present, the act of giving and receiving gifts strengthens bonds, creates lasting memories, and nurtures emotional connections. More than just material objects, gifts in relationships symbolize care, attention, and the effort one puts into making their loved one feel special.

One of the most important aspects of gift-giving is its ability to express unspoken emotions. Not everyone finds it easy to verbally articulate their feelings, and gifts can serve as a beautiful substitute for words. A handwritten letter, a thoughtfully chosen book, or a simple yet meaningful gift can convey emotions like love, gratitude, or even an apology in ways that words sometimes cannot. Gifts act as a silent language of love, communicating affection, admiration, and appreciation without the need for an elaborate speech. In this way, they become more than just physical items; they become symbols of the emotions shared between two people.

Another key role of gifts in relationships is the way they create and preserve memories. A gift is often associated with a special moment, a significant milestone, or a heartfelt gesture. Years later, looking at a particular piece of jewelry, a framed photograph, or even a stuffed teddy bear can bring back cherished memories of the day it was given. This emotional connection to gifts is what makes them so valuable in relationships—they serve as reminders of love, commitment, and shared experiences. A couple may remember the early days of their relationship through a souvenir from a trip or recall a special anniversary through a gift that marked the occasion. Such gifts hold sentimental value, making them treasures that continue to deepen the relationship over time.

Beyond sentimental value, gifts also play a role in strengthening emotional bonds and appreciation. When given with genuine intent, a gift signifies effort, attention, and the desire to make one's partner feel loved. Thoughtful gifts show that a person is attentive to their partner's likes, dislikes, and desires, demonstrating that they truly understand and care for them. A surprise gift, even something as small as a favorite snack or a heartfelt note, can brighten someone's day and reinforce feelings of appreciation. It is not the price of the gift that matters, but the thought and intention behind it.

Ultimately, the role of gifts in relationships is not about materialism but about emotional connection. Whether it is a grand gesture or a simple token, the significance of a gift lies in the emotions it carries and the meaning it holds for both the giver and the recipient. Gifts serve as reminders of love, enhance intimacy, and create shared experiences that deepen relationships. At its core, gift-giving is an act of love—one that speaks to the heart and strengthens the bond between two people, making relationships richer and more meaningful.

Creating Memories Through Softness

Love is often remembered through the moments of comfort, warmth, and tenderness that define a relationship. While grand gestures may be impressive, it is the soft, intimate moments that truly create lasting memories. The simple act of holding hands, sharing a quiet evening together, or gifting something soft and comforting—like a teddy bear—becomes embedded in the heart as a reminder of love's gentle nature. Softness, in both a literal and emotional sense, plays a vital role in strengthening relationships, providing a sense of security and affection that lasts far beyond a single moment.

A teddy bear, for example, is more than just a plush toy; it is a symbol of warmth and emotional connection. Unlike other gifts that may fade with time, a teddy bear remains, offering a source of comfort and nostalgia. Many people hold onto their teddy bears for years, not just as sentimental objects but as reminders of the person who gifted them. The softness of a teddy bear mirrors the softness of love—the way a hug can heal, the way a kind word can soothe, and the way simple gestures can make someone feel deeply cherished. This is why teddy bears are often given as symbols of reassurance, representing a love that is present even in moments of distance or solitude.

Softness also plays a role in creating meaningful memories through physical and emotional touch. A warm hug, a gentle kiss on the forehead, or the soothing sound of a partner's voice can leave an imprint on the heart, making those moments unforgettable. The human need for affection and touch is deeply connected to emotional well-being, and soft gestures reinforce the strength of love in a relationship. Even in long-distance relationships, where physical presence is limited, small tokens of softness—like a handwritten letter, a cozy blanket, or a cherished stuffed animal—can bring comfort and remind loved ones of their bond.

Beyond romantic love, softness creates memories in friendships, family relationships, and even self-love. A comforting embrace from a parent, a heartfelt note from a friend, or the warmth of a child's favorite plush toy all contribute to the emotional security that shapes lifelong connections. Softness in gestures, words, and actions fosters an environment of love and safety, where people can be their most vulnerable selves without fear. It is in these moments—when love is expressed through gentleness and care—that the most profound memories are formed.

In a world that often demands strength and resilience, love reminds us of the beauty of softness. It teaches us that tenderness is not weakness but a powerful force that binds hearts together. Whether through a cherished teddy bear, a shared embrace, or a quiet moment of understanding, the memories created through softness become the foundation of lasting relationships. They remind us that love is not just about passion and excitement but also about the quiet, reassuring presence that makes life's journey more beautiful.

Chapter 5
Promise Day – Vows of the Heart

Love is built on more than just fleeting emotions; it thrives on commitment, trust, and the promises we make to one another. Promise Day, celebrated on February 11th, is a special occasion that highlights the foundation of every strong relationship—the vows of the heart. Whether spoken or unspoken, promises serve as a testament to the depth of love and the dedication to nurturing a bond that lasts. Unlike material gifts, a promise is intangible, yet its impact is profound. It signifies a commitment to stand by each other through joys and struggles, reinforcing the idea that love is not just about passion but also about reliability, devotion, and unwavering support.

The beauty of Promise Day lies in its universality. Promises are not limited to romantic relationships; they extend to friendships, family bonds, and even personal growth. A promise to always be there, to understand, to forgive, or to cherish someone's presence can mean more than any grand gesture. Love flourishes when partners feel secure in the knowledge that they can trust and depend on one another. In a world where relationships can sometimes feel fragile, making heartfelt promises strengthens emotional connections and reassures loved ones that they are valued. These promises, whether simple or profound, become the silent threads that weave two lives together.

As we celebrate Promise Day, it is important to reflect on the significance of the commitments we make. Promises should not be empty words but sincere expressions of intent. They require effort, patience, and the willingness to nurture love even when challenges arise. Whether it is a promise to stay loyal, to communicate openly, or to support each other's dreams, each vow of the heart adds depth to a relationship. True love is not measured by grand declarations but by the quiet, everyday moments when we honor our promises, proving that love is not just a feeling—it is a choice, made every single day.

The Weight of a Promise

A promise is more than just a string of words—it is a commitment, a vow that carries the weight of trust, expectation, and responsibility. In relationships, promises form the foundation upon which love is built, shaping the depth of emotional connections and reinforcing a sense of security between two people. Whether spoken aloud or silently understood, a promise binds hearts together, creating an unspoken agreement of loyalty, care, and devotion. But with every promise made comes the responsibility of keeping it, as unfulfilled promises can weaken even the strongest bonds. The weight of a promise is not just in the words themselves but in the dedication to honoring them, proving that love is more than just emotions—it is also about integrity and action.

One of the most significant aspects of a promise is the trust it fosters. When someone makes a promise to be there, to love unconditionally, or to remain loyal, they create an emotional contract that reassures their partner that they are not alone in the journey of love. This trust becomes the backbone of a relationship, allowing both individuals to feel secure in their bond. However, broken promises, whether intentional or accidental, can lead to disappointment, doubt, and even emotional wounds that take time to heal. It is easy to make promises in moments of joy and passion, but the true strength of love is tested in moments of hardship—when fulfilling those promises requires effort, patience, and perseverance.

A promise is also a reflection of one's character and values. It is not just about making someone happy in the moment but about demonstrating reliability and consistency over time. When people uphold their promises, they show that their love is not just about words but about actions. A simple promise to listen, to be patient, or to stand by someone in difficult times can mean more than extravagant declarations of love. True commitment is not just about saying, "I will always be here for you," but proving it through presence, understanding, and unwavering support. In this way, promises become a powerful force that nurtures and strengthens love, turning it into something enduring and unshakable.

However, the weight of a promise also lies in making ones that are genuine and realistic. Love is not about making grand, unrealistic vows but about pledging things that truly matter and can be upheld with sincerity. A promise should never be made lightly, as false assurances can do more harm than good. It is better to promise less and fulfill more than to promise everything and fall short. Real promises, no matter how small, hold immense value when kept. Whether it is a promise to be honest, to support each other's dreams, or to work through difficulties together, the key is to mean every word and follow through with action.

In the end, the weight of a promise is what makes love strong, resilient, and lasting. It is a reminder that love is not just about fleeting emotions but about a lifelong commitment to being there for one another. A true promise, once made and honored, becomes the heartbeat of a relationship—steady, strong, and unwavering.

Keeping Love Strong Through Commitment

Love is often portrayed as a magical feeling that sweeps people off their feet, but in reality, love is not just about emotions—it is about commitment. While passion may ignite a relationship, it is commitment that keeps it alive. True love requires effort, patience, and the willingness to stand by each other through both joyful and challenging times. Keeping love strong is not about waiting for perfect moments; it is about making everyday moments meaningful through devotion, understanding, and shared effort. When two people commit to nurturing their love, they create a foundation that withstands the tests of time, proving that real love is not just about staying together but about growing together.

Commitment in love is demonstrated through consistent actions, not just words. It is easy to say "I love you," but true love is proven in the way people support, respect, and prioritize each other daily. This includes being present in each other's lives, making time despite busy schedules, and ensuring that love does not fade into routine. Small, thoughtful gestures—like remembering special dates, leaving a kind note, or simply asking how the other person's day went—help maintain emotional closeness. Commitment also means facing challenges as a team, rather than letting difficulties create distance. Whether it is financial struggles, career pressures, or personal insecurities, couples who are truly committed find ways to navigate hardships together instead of letting obstacles weaken their bond.

Trust and communication are two of the strongest pillars of commitment. Without trust, love becomes fragile, and without communication, misunderstandings can create emotional gaps.

Commitment requires honesty, openness, and a willingness to listen. It means discussing fears, insecurities, and expectations with transparency, rather than bottling up emotions. When both partners feel heard and understood, their connection deepens, allowing love to flourish even in the face of difficulties. Additionally, committed love is about compromise—understanding that no two individuals are the same and that differences should be embraced rather than feared. Being committed means respecting each other's individuality while working together toward a shared future.

Another vital aspect of keeping love strong is choosing love every single day. Over time, relationships evolve, and the initial excitement may settle into familiarity. This is where commitment plays its most crucial role—reminding couples that love is not just something they feel, but something they actively nurture. Committed love does not wait for grand romantic gestures to reignite passion; instead, it finds beauty in the ordinary. Holding hands during a walk, watching a favorite movie together, or sharing a meal at the end of a long day—all these moments reinforce the commitment to cherish and appreciate one another.

In the end, love is not sustained by mere words or fleeting emotions but by the actions and choices made every day. A truly committed relationship is not about perfection but about perseverance. It is about standing together, not just when love feels effortless but also when it requires patience and effort. Keeping love strong through commitment is the key to an enduring and meaningful relationship—one that is built not just on passion, but on trust, loyalty, and the unwavering decision to walk life's journey together.

Beyond Words: Living the Promise

Love is not just about the promises we make but about the way we honor and live those promises every single day. While words can be beautiful and meaningful, true love is demonstrated through actions—through the small yet powerful ways we show up for each other, support one another, and nurture our bond over time. Promises are not meant to be fleeting declarations of devotion; they are commitments that require effort, patience, and sincerity. Living the promise means embodying love, trust, and loyalty in every interaction, proving that true commitment extends far beyond spoken words.

One of the most important aspects of living a promise is consistency. In relationships, it is not enough to say "I will always be there for you" if actions do not reflect that sentiment. Love is built on reliability, on the ability to trust that a partner will be present through the highs and lows of life. This means showing up when it matters most—offering a listening ear during tough times, providing encouragement when challenges arise, and celebrating victories together, no matter how small. Living a promise means making love a priority, ensuring that the other person never feels neglected or taken for granted.

Another essential part of honoring a promise is being willing to grow and adapt. Relationships evolve, and so do the people in them. What may have been an easy promise to keep in the beginning might require more effort as life changes. Promising to love someone means embracing them as they grow, supporting their dreams, and navigating challenges together. It also means recognizing when adjustments need to be made, whether it's improving communication, working through differences, or making sacrifices for the sake of the relationship. True commitment is not about perfection; it is about the willingness to evolve while keeping love at the center.

Beyond romantic relationships, living the promise applies to friendships, family, and even the promises we make to ourselves. Promising to be there for a friend means checking in even when life gets busy. A promise to support family members means being present for them in meaningful ways. And the promises we make to ourselves—whether it is to prioritize self-care, pursue personal goals, or embrace self-love—require the same dedication and consistency as promises made to others.

Ultimately, living the promise is about turning love into action. It is about proving, through everyday gestures, that love is not just a feeling but a commitment. A partner who truly lives their promise will not just say "I love you," but will show love in the way they listen, in the way they understand, and in the way they stand by their loved one no matter what. The true beauty of a promise is not in the moment it is made, but in the countless moments that follow—moments that reaffirm its sincerity and prove that love, when nurtured with intention, can endure beyond words, beyond time, and beyond circumstance.

Chapter 6
Hug Day – The Warmth of Togetherness

Love is often best expressed not through words, but through simple, heartfelt gestures that convey deep emotions. Hug Day, celebrated on February 12th, is a celebration of warmth, comfort, and the unspoken language of love that a hug represents. A hug is more than just a physical embrace; it is a silent promise of presence, an assurance that no matter what happens, someone is there to offer support and affection. Whether between lovers, friends, family, or even strangers in moments of kindness, hugs have the power to bridge emotional gaps, heal wounds, and bring people closer in ways that words sometimes fail to do.

The act of hugging is deeply connected to emotional well-being. Studies have shown that hugs release oxytocin, the "love hormone," which reduces stress, lowers blood pressure, and strengthens feelings of trust and security. In relationships, a hug can communicate love, understanding, and forgiveness without the need for explanation. A warm embrace after a long day reassures a partner that they are valued; a comforting hug in difficult times speaks of unwavering support; a spontaneous hug in moments of joy enhances shared happiness. Hug Day reminds us that love is not only about grand romantic gestures but also about the small, meaningful moments of physical closeness that create deeper bonds.

Beyond romantic relationships, Hug Day encourages the celebration of love in all its forms. A hug from a parent to a child provides a sense of protection and unconditional love, while a hug between friends strengthens trust and connection. Even self-hugs—embracing oneself with kindness and self-compassion—are a powerful reminder of self-love and acceptance. As we celebrate this day, we recognize that a simple hug can brighten someone's mood, dissolve feelings of loneliness, and bring warmth into our lives. It is a universal gesture of love that needs no translation, reminding us that sometimes, the best way to express love is simply to hold someone close and let them feel it.

The Science of a Loving Embrace

A hug is often seen as a simple, instinctive act of affection, but beneath its warmth lies a profound scientific impact on the mind and body. More than just a gesture of love, a hug triggers a complex physiological response that promotes emotional well-being, reduces stress, and strengthens human connections. Science has long supported the idea that physical touch, especially through hugs, plays a crucial role in mental and physical health. Whether it's a comforting embrace from a loved one, a reassuring hug between friends, or a spontaneous moment of connection, the act of hugging influences our emotions and strengthens bonds in ways that words cannot.

One of the most significant benefits of hugging is the release of oxytocin, commonly referred to as the "love hormone" or the "bonding hormone." Oxytocin is a neuropeptide that enhances feelings of trust, security, and attachment. When we hug someone, our brain signals the release of oxytocin, which in turn lowers cortisol levels, the hormone responsible for stress. This hormonal shift creates a sense of calm, reduces anxiety, and promotes a feeling of connection. Oxytocin is especially important in romantic relationships, as it fosters emotional intimacy and strengthens the bond between partners. The more frequently couples hug and engage in affectionate touch, the stronger their emotional connection tends to be.

Beyond emotional well-being, hugging also has significant physical health benefits. Studies have shown that regular physical touch, including hugs, can lower blood pressure and heart rate, reducing the risk of heart disease. This is because hugs activate the parasympathetic nervous system, which helps the body relax and recover from stress. Additionally, the warmth of an embrace increases serotonin and dopamine levels—neurotransmitters associated with happiness and pleasure—leading to improved mood and emotional resilience. Hugging has even been linked to improved immune function, as it helps regulate stress levels that can weaken the immune system.

The power of a hug extends beyond romantic relationships and into social connections as well. Hugging promotes a sense of belonging and security, reinforcing bonds between family members, friends, and even communities. In times of grief or distress, a hug can provide comfort and reassurance, communicating empathy without the need for words. The simple act of holding someone close lets them know they are not alone, making hugs an essential part of human connection. This is especially true for children, as physical touch in early development plays a crucial role in forming healthy emotional attachments and boosting self-esteem.

Even self-hugging—a concept often overlooked—can have powerful psychological benefits. Wrapping one's arms around oneself in a moment of distress or self-doubt can provide a sense of comfort and reassurance. Practicing self-compassion through touch helps reinforce positive self-worth and emotional healing.

Ultimately, the science of a loving embrace proves that hugs are far more than just acts of affection; they are essential to emotional and physical well-being. Whether shared between partners, friends, or family members, a heartfelt hug fosters love, reduces stress, and nurtures relationships, making it one of the simplest yet most powerful expressions of human connection.

Hugs That Heal: Emotional and Physical Connection

Hugs are one of the most natural and powerful ways to express love, support, and reassurance. While they may seem like simple gestures, hugs hold an incredible ability to heal both emotionally and physically. A heartfelt embrace can provide comfort in times of distress, strengthen relationships, and even improve overall well-being. Whether it is a warm hug from a loved one after a long day or a supportive embrace during a difficult moment, hugs create a deep sense of connection that transcends words. Science and psychology both confirm that hugs have tangible benefits, reinforcing the idea that physical touch is essential for emotional and physical health.

Emotionally, hugs provide a sense of security and belonging. When we embrace someone, it signals safety and reassurance, helping to ease anxiety and stress. Hugs release oxytocin, also known as the "love hormone" or the "cuddle hormone," which enhances feelings of trust and bonding. This hormone plays a crucial role in strengthening relationships, whether between romantic partners, family members, or friends. A simple hug can make someone feel valued, understood, and supported, making it one of the most effective ways to communicate love and empathy without words.

Beyond emotional comfort, hugs also offer significant physical benefits. Research has shown that regular hugging can help lower blood pressure and heart rate, reducing the risk of cardiovascular disease. The physical act of hugging activates the parasympathetic nervous system, which helps the body relax and recover from stress. Additionally, hugs reduce cortisol levels, the hormone responsible for stress, which can have a profound impact on mental health. People who receive frequent hugs tend to experience lower levels of depression and anxiety, as physical touch plays a crucial role in emotional regulation and well-being.

Hugs also have a powerful impact on the immune system. Studies suggest that people who receive regular hugs are less likely to fall sick, as the reduction in stress contributes to stronger immune function. The warmth and pressure of a hug stimulate the vagus nerve, which helps regulate bodily functions and promotes overall health. In moments of physical pain, hugs can also provide relief by releasing endorphins, the body's natural painkillers, creating a sense of comfort and relaxation.

The healing power of hugs is not limited to romantic or familial relationships—it extends to friendships, communities, and even self-care. During moments of grief or sadness, a hug can be more comforting than words, offering silent support and emotional healing. Even self-hugging, a practice of wrapping one's arms around oneself, can provide a sense of comfort and reassurance, especially during times of loneliness or self-doubt.

Ultimately, hugs are more than just gestures; they are an essential part of human connection. They remind us that love and care can be communicated through the simplest touch, reinforcing the importance of presence, warmth, and support in our lives. Whether shared in moments of joy, sorrow, or daily affection, hugs serve as a universal language of healing, strengthening both emotional and physical bonds in profound ways.

When Actions Speak Louder Than Words

Love is often expressed through words, but it is truly defined by actions. While verbal affirmations like "I love you" and "I'm here for you" hold meaning, they are only as powerful as the actions that accompany them. In relationships, both romantic and otherwise, actions serve as the real testament to one's feelings, commitment, and sincerity. When words fade, it is the consistent, thoughtful gestures — small and grand — that strengthen bonds, build trust, and create lasting memories. Actions have the ability to communicate love, reassurance, and dedication in ways that words alone cannot.

One of the most significant ways that actions speak louder than words is through consistency. Anyone can make promises, but love is demonstrated in the way those promises are upheld over time. A person who truly cares does not just say they will always be there — they show it through their presence, patience, and unwavering support. A hug after a stressful day, a spontaneous act of kindness, or simply remembering small details about a loved one's life can mean more than repeated declarations of love. In contrast, when actions do not align with words, trust begins to erode. Saying "I'll always be there" but failing to show up when needed weakens the emotional connection, making words feel empty.

Another way actions surpass words is through sacrifices and selflessness. Love often requires putting someone else's needs ahead of one's own, even in small ways. Whether it is making time despite a busy schedule, offering help without being asked, or being there during difficult times, selfless actions strengthen relationships. A person who genuinely loves someone does not just express affection in moments of joy but also stands beside them in moments of struggle. Love is about showing up when it is inconvenient, about proving that someone's well-being matters, not just when things are easy, but when they are challenging.

Non-verbal communication also plays a crucial role in expressing love and care. Gestures, body language, and touch often convey emotions more powerfully than spoken words. A comforting embrace, holding hands during a difficult conversation, or a reassuring look can communicate love and understanding without a single word being spoken. In many cases, physical affection—such as hugs, kisses, or even small touches—can ease pain, reduce stress, and strengthen intimacy in ways that words simply cannot replicate.

At its core, love is an experience, not just a sentiment. It is something felt in the way two people interact, in the moments of laughter, in the silent support, and in the everyday gestures that make life richer. Words can create a foundation, but it is actions that build the structure of a lasting relationship. The true test of love is not in what is said, but in what is consistently done. In the end, actions become the proof of love's authenticity, reminding us that while words can express love, it is through actions that love is truly lived and felt.

Chapter 7
Kiss Day – The Silent Expression of Love

A kiss is one of the most intimate and profound expressions of love, transcending words and speaking directly to the heart. Kiss Day, celebrated on February 13th, is dedicated to this beautiful act of affection, symbolizing love, passion, and emotional closeness. A kiss can convey emotions that words often fail to capture—whether it is the excitement of a first kiss, the warmth of a gentle peck, or the deep connection of a passionate embrace. Across cultures and throughout history, kisses have held deep significance, representing love, respect, devotion, and even promises of forever. More than just a physical act, a kiss is a silent language of the heart, a moment where two souls connect without the need for words.

The power of a kiss lies not just in its physical sensation but in the emotions and intentions behind it. A soft kiss on the forehead expresses care and protection, a kiss on the cheek signifies friendship and admiration, while a lingering kiss between lovers strengthens intimacy and trust. Scientific studies have even shown that kissing releases a rush of endorphins, dopamine, and oxytocin—the same hormones associated with happiness, love, and emotional bonding. In this way, a kiss is more than just an expression of romance; it is a biological and emotional bridge that strengthens relationships and deepens connections.

Kiss Day serves as a reminder of the magic that exists in simple yet meaningful gestures of love. In the rush of everyday life, it is easy to overlook these small moments of affection, yet they are often the ones that sustain and nurture a relationship. A kiss can rekindle passion, heal emotional wounds, and offer reassurance in ways that go beyond spoken promises. Whether shared between lovers, family members, or friends, a kiss remains a universal symbol of love and connection. As we celebrate this day, we embrace the beauty of love's silent expression and the timeless power of a kiss to convey what words sometimes cannot.

The Power of a Kiss in Romance

A kiss is one of the most intimate and powerful gestures in a romantic relationship, capable of expressing emotions that words often fail to convey. It is a silent yet profound declaration of love, passion, desire, and commitment. Whether it is a gentle peck, a lingering embrace, or a passionate kiss, this simple act strengthens the bond between two people, deepening their connection both emotionally and physically. Throughout history, literature, and science, the significance of a kiss has been explored and celebrated as a universal expression of love, making it one of the most cherished moments in romance.

One of the reasons why a kiss holds such power in romance is its ability to strengthen emotional intimacy. A kiss is not just a physical act; it is a way of saying, "I see you, I cherish you, and I desire to be close to you." When two people kiss, they share an unspoken understanding, a moment of vulnerability where emotions are exchanged without the need for words. The connection built through kissing goes beyond attraction—it fosters trust, affection, and reassurance in a relationship. A single kiss can melt away doubts, soothe insecurities, and reaffirm the love between two individuals.

Scientifically, kissing triggers the release of hormones that enhance love and happiness. When two people kiss, their brains release oxytocin, dopamine, and serotonin—hormones associated with bonding, pleasure, and emotional connection. Oxytocin, often called the "love hormone," strengthens feelings of attachment and trust, reinforcing the emotional bond between partners. Dopamine creates a sense of euphoria and excitement, which explains why a passionate kiss can feel exhilarating. Meanwhile, serotonin helps elevate mood, reducing stress and anxiety. This biochemical reaction not only enhances the romantic experience but also contributes to overall relationship satisfaction and emotional well-being.

Beyond emotional and scientific aspects, a kiss also plays a crucial role in maintaining and reigniting passion in a relationship. Over time, as relationships mature, partners may fall into routines where affection is expressed less frequently. However, a meaningful kiss can reignite the spark, reminding both individuals of the passion and attraction that brought them together in the first place. A deep kiss can rekindle lost intimacy, creating a moment where time seems to stop, and only love exists. It serves as a reminder that romance is not just about grand gestures but also about the small yet significant moments of closeness.

Kissing is also a universal language of love, transcending cultural, linguistic, and emotional barriers. Across the world, couples share kisses as a way of expressing their deepest emotions, whether it is a kiss of greeting, farewell, or devotion. From the first kiss that sparks a love story to the affectionate kisses exchanged over years of companionship, this simple act continues to play an essential role in the journey of love.

Ultimately, the power of a kiss in romance lies in its ability to create an intimate connection, evoke deep emotions, and strengthen the foundation of love. A kiss is more than just an act of affection—it is a moment of unity, passion, and silent understanding that binds two hearts together in the most beautiful way possible.

The Language of Intimacy

Intimacy is more than just physical closeness; it is a deep emotional connection that binds two people together in a way that transcends words. While love can be spoken, true intimacy is often communicated through silent gestures, shared moments, and unspoken understanding. Among these, kissing stands as one of the most profound expressions of intimacy, a language in itself that conveys emotions, passion, trust, and vulnerability. A kiss is not just an act of affection but a bridge that connects two souls, strengthening their bond and deepening their love.

In relationships, intimacy is built over time through shared experiences, mutual trust, and the willingness to be emotionally open with one another. A kiss, whether tender or passionate, speaks volumes about the depth of a relationship. A soft kiss on the forehead conveys protection and care, a lingering kiss on the lips expresses desire and devotion, and a stolen kiss in a quiet moment signifies the joy of connection. These intimate gestures foster a sense of security and belonging, making both partners feel seen, valued, and cherished. Unlike words, which can sometimes be misunderstood or misinterpreted, the language of intimacy through touch and affection is raw and honest, leaving no room for doubt.

The power of intimacy through a kiss also lies in its ability to create an emotional sanctuary—a space where love is felt deeply without the need for explanation. When two people kiss, their bodies release oxytocin, also known as the "bonding hormone," which enhances trust and attachment. This chemical reaction reinforces emotional closeness, making partners feel more connected to each other. Beyond the physical sensations, a kiss creates a moment where two people share their innermost emotions, allowing them to be vulnerable and open without fear of rejection. This is why a meaningful kiss can heal misunderstandings, reignite passion, and serve as a reminder of the love that brought two people together.

The language of intimacy is not just about passion but also about emotional reassurance. In moments of sadness, a gentle kiss on the forehead can provide comfort. After a long day, a warm embrace followed by a kiss can ease stress and anxiety. These gestures remind partners that they are not alone, that their emotions are acknowledged and understood. Intimacy thrives on these small, consistent acts of love, proving that closeness is not just about physical attraction but about creating a bond that is both emotional and spiritual.

Ultimately, intimacy is about connection, and kissing is one of its most beautiful expressions. It is a reminder that love is not just about words or grand gestures, but about the quiet, meaningful moments shared between two hearts. Whether in a new romance or a long-term relationship, the language of intimacy remains timeless—spoken through the touch of a hand, the warmth of a kiss, and the deep understanding that love is not just felt but also expressed in the simplest and most powerful ways.

Cherishing Moments of Passion

Passion is one of the most exhilarating and transformative aspects of love. It is the spark that ignites attraction, the energy that fuels intimacy, and the force that keeps relationships vibrant and alive. While love provides stability and comfort, passion adds excitement and depth, making every shared moment feel intense and meaningful. Cherishing moments of passion means recognizing the power of these experiences, embracing them fully, and nurturing them to strengthen the emotional and physical connection between two people. Passion is not just about physical intimacy; it is about emotional closeness, desire, and the willingness to be completely present in each other's lives.

In the early stages of a relationship, passion often comes naturally. The excitement of new love brings an undeniable intensity—every touch, every look, every kiss feels electric. These moments are fueled by anticipation and curiosity, as partners explore and discover each other's emotions, thoughts, and desires. However, as relationships mature, passion may shift from fiery intensity to a deeper, more meaningful connection. This does not mean passion fades; rather, it evolves. The key to cherishing moments of passion is to continuously nurture them, ensuring that love remains exciting, intimate, and deeply fulfilling.

One of the most powerful ways to keep passion alive is by being fully present in romantic moments. In today's fast-paced world, distractions often take away from the ability to truly connect. Work, technology, and daily responsibilities can make couples lose sight of the passion that brought them together in the first place. By making a conscious effort to be present—whether during a deep conversation, a romantic dinner, or a simple embrace—partners can reignite their emotional and physical bond. Passion flourishes when both individuals are engaged, attentive, and committed to making each other feel desired and valued.

Beyond physical affection, passion is also about emotional connection and appreciation. Taking the time to express admiration, complimenting each other, and reminding one another of their unique qualities helps sustain passion in a relationship. Love should never become routine; instead, it should be filled with small, intentional acts that reinforce desire and appreciation. Surprising a partner with an affectionate note, planning a spontaneous date, or recreating a special memory can reignite the excitement and joy of being together. Passion is about making love feel new, no matter how many years pass.

At its core, cherishing moments of passion means never taking love for granted. It means recognizing that passion is not just something that happens—it is something that is created, nurtured, and celebrated. Whether it is through a meaningful kiss, a lingering touch, or a shared adventure, passion is what keeps relationships exciting and alive. By making an effort to embrace passion, couples can deepen their connection, create lasting memories, and continue to fall in love with each other, over and over again. Love is a journey, and passion is the fire that makes it unforgettable.

Chapter 8
Valentine's Day – The Celebration of Eternal Love

Valentine's Day, celebrated on February 14th, is more than just a day of chocolates, flowers, and romantic gestures—it is a celebration of love in its purest and most enduring form. Across the world, people take this day to express their feelings, cherish their loved ones, and reaffirm the bonds they share. Whether it is through heartfelt words, thoughtful gifts, or simple moments of togetherness, Valentine's Day serves as a reminder that love is a timeless force that brings people closer. While the traditions may differ from culture to culture, the essence remains the same: love is meant to be celebrated, nurtured, and treasured, not just for a single day but for a lifetime.

Beyond the grand gestures and romantic dates, the true significance of Valentine's Day lies in its emotional depth. It is not just about couples in love; it is a day to appreciate all forms of love—between friends, family, and even self-love. Love is the foundation of human connection, and Valentine's Day provides an opportunity to reflect on the relationships that bring meaning to life. In a world that often moves too fast, this day encourages people to pause and express gratitude for those who stand by them, offering love, support, and companionship through life's journey.

At its heart, Valentine's Day is a celebration of eternal love, the kind that withstands time, distance, and challenges. True love is not defined by fleeting moments but by the continuous effort to care, understand, and support one another. Whether it is the excitement of new love, the comfort of a long-term relationship, or the deep bond shared between family and friends, Valentine's Day serves as a reminder that love is the most beautiful and enduring force in the world. As we celebrate this day, we embrace the idea that love is not meant to be confined to a single date on the calendar—it is a commitment, a feeling, and a promise that lasts forever.

Beyond Grand Gestures: The True Meaning of Love

Love is often portrayed through grand gestures—extravagant gifts, candlelit dinners, and public displays of affection. While these expressions of love are beautiful and meaningful, they are not the foundation of true love. Love is not measured by the size of a bouquet or the price of a gift but by the everyday moments of care, understanding, and commitment. The true meaning of love lies in the small, consistent acts that strengthen a relationship over time, proving that love is not just about fleeting excitement but about deep, unwavering connection.

At its core, love is about presence and effort. It is in the way two people show up for each other, not just in joyful moments but in times of struggle, uncertainty, and hardship. A grand romantic surprise may be memorable, but what truly sustains love is the ability to support and uplift one another through life's challenges. A simple text to check in, a reassuring touch after a long day, or the patience to listen when the other needs to be heard—these small gestures hold far greater value than any grand display. Love is about consistency, about choosing to nurture the relationship even when life gets busy or difficult.

True love is also about understanding and acceptance. It is not about perfection or fairy-tale romance; it is about embracing each other's flaws, quirks, and vulnerabilities. Real love does not demand constant excitement or extravagant gifts; it thrives on honesty, emotional safety, and deep connection. It is found in the moments of laughter over inside jokes, in the comfortable silences where words are not needed, and in the trust that allows two people to be their authentic selves. Love is not about changing someone to fit an ideal but about accepting and cherishing them exactly as they are.

Moreover, love is about sacrifice and compromise. It is not just about personal happiness but about considering the needs and feelings of a partner. Love means making sacrifices, big or small, to bring happiness and comfort to the one you care about. It means compromising, not because you have to, but because you want to see the other person happy. Love is found in the willingness to adjust, to grow together, and to prioritize each other's well-being. It is not about keeping score but about giving freely, without expecting anything in return.

Ultimately, the true meaning of love is found in the everyday moments, in the way two people make each other feel loved, valued, and understood. Love is not about proving affection through grand acts; it is about proving it through patience, kindness, and unwavering support. It is in the way two people share their dreams, face their fears, and build a life together, brick by brick, with love as the foundation. Grand gestures may be fleeting, but real love—the kind that lasts—lives in the small, quiet moments that truly matter.

Making Every Day Special

Love is not just about celebrating grand occasions like Valentine's Day, anniversaries, or birthdays; it is about cherishing each day and making ordinary moments feel extraordinary. While special events serve as reminders to express love, true romance lies in the effort to make every single day meaningful. Love thrives not in occasional grand gestures but in the small, everyday acts of kindness, appreciation, and thoughtfulness that strengthen relationships over time. When love is nurtured daily, it becomes a source of constant joy, security, and connection, proving that the most beautiful relationships are not built on occasional celebrations but on continuous effort and care.

One of the best ways to make every day special is through small, thoughtful gestures. A simple "good morning" message, a warm hug before leaving for the day, or a heartfelt compliment can instantly brighten a loved one's mood. It's not always about expensive gifts or extravagant plans—it's about showing appreciation through meaningful actions. Preparing a partner's favorite meal, leaving a sweet note on their desk, or remembering the little things that make them smile can turn even the most ordinary day into something memorable. Love flourishes when both partners feel seen, valued, and appreciated, and these small acts of care reinforce that they matter every single day.

Another essential part of making every day special is spending quality time together. In the hustle and bustle of daily life, it's easy to let routines take over and forget to nurture the emotional connection in a relationship. However, love needs time and attention to grow. Setting aside time to talk without distractions, watching a favorite show together, or taking a walk while holding hands can strengthen the bond between two people. It doesn't have to be elaborate—what matters is the intention behind it. Shared experiences, no matter how simple, help create lasting memories and deepen intimacy.

Surprising one another in small ways can also keep love exciting and fresh. A surprise date night, an unexpected gift, or even a spontaneous adventure can bring joy to a relationship and break the monotony of daily life. Surprises do not always have to be planned — they can be as simple as sending a loving message during the day, playing a song that holds special meaning, or reminiscing about happy memories together. These little surprises remind both partners that love is something to be celebrated every day, not just on special occasions.

Most importantly, making every day special requires emotional presence and attentiveness. It's about listening when a partner speaks, offering support when they need it, and being a steady source of love and encouragement. A loving relationship is not about perfection but about the willingness to make an effort, to be kind, and to create moments of happiness together. When two people prioritize each other, making each day special becomes a natural part of their relationship.

In the end, love is not about waiting for grand milestones — it is about appreciating the journey and making every moment count. A strong relationship is built on the foundation of everyday love, where both partners commit to cherishing, celebrating, and valuing each other in both the extraordinary and the ordinary.

Building a Love That Lasts

Love, at its core, is not just about fleeting emotions or passionate moments — it is about creating something enduring, something that stands the test of time. While falling in love may happen effortlessly, staying in love requires dedication, patience, and a mutual commitment to growing together. A lasting love is built on trust, communication, and a shared vision for the future. It is not about perfection but about embracing imperfections, overcoming challenges, and continuously choosing each other, day after day.

One of the most essential pillars of lasting love is trust. A relationship without trust is like a house built on a weak foundation—it may stand for a while, but it will eventually crumble under pressure. Trust is developed through honesty, consistency, and reliability. It means being open about feelings, sharing vulnerabilities, and proving through actions that one's love and commitment are unwavering. In strong relationships, partners feel secure in each other's love, knowing they can rely on one another in times of joy and hardship. Trust does not happen overnight; it is built over time through meaningful interactions and genuine care.

Effective communication is another key element in building a love that lasts. Many relationships struggle not because of a lack of love but because of misunderstandings and unresolved conflicts. Healthy communication involves not just talking but also actively listening, understanding, and respecting each other's perspectives. It means expressing needs without fear, addressing concerns with kindness, and finding solutions together rather than allowing resentment to build. When couples communicate openly and honestly, they create an environment where love can flourish without the barriers of doubt or misinterpretation.

Another crucial aspect of long-lasting love is adaptability and growth. No relationship remains the same over time; both individuals evolve, and so must the relationship. Couples who embrace change and grow together are more likely to sustain their love. This means supporting each other's dreams, being open to new experiences, and adjusting to life's inevitable shifts. A love that lasts is one that adapts—one where partners encourage each other's personal development while maintaining their connection. Growth in love does not mean never facing difficulties; it means working through them with a shared commitment to staying together.

Acts of love and appreciation also play a vital role in keeping love strong. The small, everyday gestures—such as expressing gratitude, offering a comforting touch, or remembering the little things that make a partner happy—help reinforce emotional bonds. Love should not be taken for granted; it should be nurtured through kindness, patience, and intentional actions. Celebrating each other, finding joy in the little things, and continuously making an effort to make the relationship special keeps love alive and thriving.

Ultimately, building a love that lasts is about choosing love every day. It is about being there through the ups and downs, embracing both the beauty and the struggles, and committing to making the relationship stronger with each passing moment. When love is nurtured with care, respect, and devotion, it becomes a force that can withstand time, distance, and challenges—creating a bond that is truly unbreakable.

Chapter 9
Love Beyond Romance – Strengthening Every Relationship

Love is often associated with romance, passion, and grand gestures, but its true essence extends far beyond romantic relationships. Love exists in many forms—between friends, family, mentors, and even within communities—each playing a vital role in shaping our emotional well-being and sense of belonging. While Valentine's Week is traditionally celebrated as a romantic occasion, it is also an opportunity to acknowledge and cherish the love that exists in all aspects of life. Strengthening these relationships fosters deeper connections, creating a world where love is not limited to couples but is instead a shared experience among all who care for one another.

The love between friends is one of the most beautiful and enduring connections in life. Friendships are built on trust, support, and shared experiences, offering a safe space to be oneself without fear of judgment. A true friend is there to celebrate successes, offer comfort during hardships, and provide a listening ear when needed. Similarly, familial love—between parents, siblings, and extended family—forms the foundation of our earliest experiences with affection and security. Strengthening these relationships requires time, patience, and effort, but the rewards are immeasurable, as they provide a sense of stability and unwavering support throughout life's journey.

Beyond personal relationships, love can also be found in acts of kindness and compassion toward others. Love is not just about receiving; it is about giving—offering warmth to a stranger, supporting a cause, or simply being present for someone in need. Whether through mentorship, community service, or small daily gestures, expressing love beyond romance helps create a more connected and empathetic world. As we celebrate love in all its forms, we realize that true love is not confined to romantic partnerships—it is a universal force that strengthens every relationship, making life more meaningful and fulfilling.

The Beauty of Platonic Love

Love is often associated with romance, passion, and attraction, but some of the deepest and most meaningful connections in life come from platonic love. Platonic love is the purest form of affection, built on trust, companionship, and mutual respect, without the expectations of romance or physical intimacy. It is the love between close friends, soul connections, and kindred spirits—those who understand, support, and cherish each other unconditionally. While romantic love may come and go, platonic love often lasts a lifetime, providing comfort, emotional security, and a sense of belonging in an ever-changing world.

One of the greatest beauties of platonic love is the freedom it brings. Unlike romantic relationships, which often come with commitments and expectations, platonic love is based purely on emotional connection. It allows people to love and care for each other without the complications of romance, making space for deep conversations, shared experiences, and an unbreakable bond. True friends who share platonic love do not demand exclusivity or expect constant validation; instead, they provide unwavering support, knowing that their connection is strong enough to withstand time and distance. In a world where relationships can sometimes feel conditional, platonic love offers a rare and refreshing kind of companionship.

Another significant aspect of platonic love is its role in emotional well-being. Friends who share a deep platonic connection provide a safe space to express emotions without fear of judgment. They celebrate successes, help navigate hardships, and offer honest advice when needed. These relationships become a source of strength, reducing stress, loneliness, and anxiety. Studies have even shown that strong friendships can improve mental health and overall happiness. In moments of doubt or despair, knowing that someone genuinely cares—without expectations of anything in return—can be profoundly healing. Platonic love proves that true intimacy is not about romance; it is about understanding and accepting someone completely.

Platonic love also challenges societal expectations and redefines the meaning of deep relationships. Often, love is categorized into rigid definitions—romantic or familial—but platonic love blurs those boundaries, showing that deep connections are not limited to partners or family members. A person may find a soulmate in a best friend, a life companion in a mentor, or an unshakable bond with someone they met unexpectedly. These relationships remind us that love is vast and infinite, existing in many forms beyond what traditional narratives suggest.

Ultimately, the beauty of platonic love lies in its unconditional nature. It is a love that asks for nothing but gives everything—

understanding, laughter, companionship, and loyalty. It teaches us that love is not defined by labels or expectations but by the depth of care we share with others. Whether through childhood friendships, deep bonds formed in adulthood, or lifelong connections that withstand time, platonic love is one of the most fulfilling and enriching experiences in life. It is a reminder that love does not always have to be romantic to be profound—it just has to be genuine.

Expressing Gratitude in Everyday Bonds

Gratitude is one of the most powerful ways to strengthen relationships and nurture deeper connections with those we love. Whether it is with a romantic partner, a close friend, a family member, or even a colleague, expressing gratitude can transform everyday interactions into meaningful moments. Love is not just about grand gestures or special occasions; it is about appreciating the presence, effort, and kindness of those around us. When we actively show gratitude in our relationships, we reinforce the importance of those bonds, making the people in our lives feel valued, respected, and cherished.

One of the simplest yet most impactful ways to express gratitude is through words. A heartfelt "thank you" can go a long way in making someone feel appreciated. Acknowledging the little things—whether it is a friend who always listens, a partner who supports our dreams, or a parent who never stops caring—creates a sense of warmth and recognition. Sometimes, we assume that our loved ones know how much they mean to us, but verbalizing our gratitude strengthens our relationships. Taking a moment to say, "I appreciate you" or "I'm grateful for everything you do," can brighten someone's day and reinforce the love we share.

Beyond words, gratitude is most powerful when expressed through actions. Simple gestures such as leaving a thoughtful note, giving a warm hug, or making time for someone despite a busy schedule demonstrate appreciation in ways that words alone cannot. Showing gratitude can be as small as preparing a loved one's favorite meal, helping with a task without being asked, or simply being present when they need support. These little acts of kindness show that we recognize and appreciate the effort others put into our lives. The key to maintaining strong bonds is making gratitude a habit, not just an occasional act.

Another meaningful way to express gratitude is through active listening and acknowledgment. Often, people just want to feel heard and understood. Paying full attention when someone speaks, remembering details about their life, and recognizing their emotions all contribute to a deeper bond. When we listen with intention and acknowledge someone's presence, we communicate that they matter to us. A simple, "I see how hard you're working" or "I admire your strength" makes people feel valued and reinforces a sense of connection.

Expressing gratitude also has a profound impact on our own well-being. Studies have shown that people who regularly practice gratitude experience higher levels of happiness, reduced stress, and stronger relationships. When we focus on the positives in our relationships rather than dwelling on imperfections, we cultivate an environment of love and appreciation. Gratitude helps shift our perspective from what is lacking to what is abundant, allowing us to see the beauty in the connections we have.

Ultimately, love is not just about big romantic gestures or material gifts; it is about appreciation, recognition, and kindness.

When we make the effort to express gratitude in our everyday bonds, we deepen our relationships and create a culture of love and appreciation. Whether through words, actions, or simply being there, gratitude strengthens the foundation of every relationship, making life richer and more meaningful for everyone involved.

Love as a Universal Language

Love is the one emotion that transcends all barriers—language, culture, geography, and even time. It is a force that unites people across the world, proving that, despite our differences, we all share the same fundamental need for connection, care, and understanding. Love does not require words to be understood; it is expressed through actions, gestures, and emotions that speak to the heart. Whether it is the love between family members, the deep connection between friends, or the passion shared between partners, love remains a universal language that binds humanity together in its most profound form.

One of the most beautiful aspects of love is that it exists in countless forms, yet its essence remains unchanged. A mother's love for her child in one part of the world is no different from a mother's love elsewhere. The friendship shared between two people in one country mirrors the friendships found in another. Romantic love, despite cultural differences, follows the same emotions of longing, devotion, and affection. Love is not confined to a single definition; it is fluid, adapting to different relationships and circumstances while still carrying the same depth and significance. This is what makes love universal—it is felt and understood by everyone, regardless of background or beliefs.

The universality of love is also evident in the way it is expressed beyond words. Love is not limited to verbal declarations; it is conveyed through a warm embrace, a gentle touch, a kind gesture, or even a simple smile. In many cultures, love is expressed through acts of service—cooking a meal for a loved one, offering help without being asked, or simply being present when someone is in need. In other cultures, love is celebrated through music, dance, and traditions that reinforce emotional connections. Despite the differences in expression, the underlying message is always the same: love is about caring for someone, wanting their happiness, and being there for them.

Beyond personal relationships, love is also the foundation of human compassion and empathy. Acts of kindness—whether helping a stranger, showing generosity, or advocating for others—are all forms of love in action. Humanitarian efforts, charitable work, and the willingness to support those in need are reflections of love's universal reach. Love inspires people to break barriers, extend kindness beyond their immediate circles, and create positive change in the world. When we act with love, we contribute to a more connected and compassionate society.

Ultimately, love is what makes us human. It is the force that drives us to build relationships, seek understanding, and find meaning in our lives. While languages and traditions may differ, the need for love is the same everywhere. It is the language that requires no translation, the feeling that unites us all, and the most powerful force that shapes our experiences. In a world that is often divided by differences, love remains the one truth that connects every heart, proving that, in the end, we are all bound by the same universal language.

Chapter 10
The Role of Self-Love – Embracing Your Own Heart

Love is often thought of as something we give to others—our family, friends, and romantic partners. However, one of the most important yet overlooked aspects of love is self-love. Before we can fully love and support others, we must first cultivate love and kindness toward ourselves. Self-love is not about arrogance or selfishness; it is about understanding our worth, valuing our well-being, and treating ourselves with the same compassion and care that we extend to those we love. When we embrace our own hearts, we develop a stronger sense of confidence, inner peace, and emotional resilience, allowing us to build healthier relationships with those around us.

Self-love is essential because it influences the way we navigate life, handle challenges, and interact with others. When we practice self-love, we set healthy boundaries, prioritize our mental and physical health, and make choices that align with our values and happiness. It helps us recognize toxic patterns, avoid relationships that diminish our self-worth, and embrace connections that uplift and empower us. A person who truly loves themselves does not seek validation from external sources but instead finds fulfillment from within, making them more emotionally secure and capable of giving love freely and authentically.

In a world that often emphasizes perfection and external validation, embracing self-love can be challenging. Society constantly presents unrealistic standards of success, beauty, and happiness, making many people feel as though they are not enough. However, self-love is about accepting oneself fully—the strengths, the flaws, and everything in between. It is about showing kindness to oneself, forgiving past mistakes, and celebrating personal growth. When we learn to embrace our own hearts, we cultivate a deeper sense of joy and fulfillment, allowing love to flourish in every aspect of our lives.

The Importance of Loving Yourself

Loving yourself is not just an act of self-care; it is a fundamental necessity for a fulfilling and meaningful life. While love is often associated with relationships with others, the relationship we have with ourselves is the foundation for all other connections. When we cultivate self-love, we develop a stronger sense of confidence, inner peace, and emotional resilience, allowing us to navigate life's challenges with grace and strength. Self-love is not about vanity or selfishness; it is about recognizing our worth, embracing our imperfections, and treating ourselves with the same kindness and compassion that we offer to those we love.

One of the most important aspects of self-love is self-acceptance. Many people struggle with feelings of inadequacy, comparing themselves to societal standards of success, beauty, and happiness. This constant pursuit of external validation can lead to self-doubt and dissatisfaction. However, true self-love comes from within—it is about accepting who you are, with all your strengths and flaws, and understanding that you are enough just as you are. When we love ourselves, we stop seeking approval from others and instead find validation from our own sense of self-worth. This leads to a greater sense of confidence and a more authentic way of living.

Self-love also plays a crucial role in mental and emotional well-being. When we neglect ourselves, whether by engaging in negative self-talk, overworking, or ignoring our own needs, we create an environment where stress, anxiety, and self-doubt thrive. Practicing self-love means setting healthy boundaries, prioritizing rest, and engaging in activities that bring joy and fulfillment. It also means being kind to oneself in times of failure or disappointment. Instead of harsh self-criticism, self-love encourages a mindset of growth—understanding that mistakes are opportunities for learning rather than reasons for self-punishment. By nurturing self-compassion, we develop greater emotional resilience and a more positive outlook on life.

Another reason self-love is so important is that it influences the way we experience relationships. When we do not love ourselves, we may find ourselves in unhealthy relationships, settling for less than we deserve, or allowing others to treat us poorly. However, when we practice self-love, we set higher standards for how we are treated and attract relationships that are based on mutual respect and care. Loving yourself also means being comfortable with solitude, understanding that your happiness does not depend on someone else but is something you create for yourself. This self-sufficiency leads to stronger, healthier relationships, as love is given and received freely rather than out of need or insecurity.

Ultimately, loving yourself is the key to a fulfilling and balanced life. It allows you to embrace your journey with confidence, handle challenges with resilience, and build relationships that are rooted in respect and authenticity. When you truly love yourself, you radiate a positive energy that not only improves your own life but also inspires and uplifts those around you. Self-love is not a destination but a continuous practice—one that, when nurtured, creates a deep and lasting sense of joy, fulfillment, and inner peace.

Self-Care as an Act of Love

Self-care is often seen as a luxury or an occasional indulgence, but in reality, it is one of the most profound ways we can express love for ourselves. Just as we nurture and care for the people we love, we must also extend that same compassion, patience, and kindness to ourselves. Self-care is not selfish; it is an essential act of self-love that allows us to maintain emotional, physical, and mental well-being. When we take care of ourselves, we not only improve our own lives but also become better partners, friends, and family members, capable of giving love more fully and freely.

One of the most important aspects of self-care is prioritizing mental and emotional well-being. In a world that constantly demands productivity, it is easy to neglect our emotional needs, pushing aside rest, relaxation, and self-reflection in favor of meeting external expectations. However, true self-care involves setting boundaries, taking breaks when needed, and allowing ourselves time to process emotions. Engaging in mindfulness, meditation, journaling, or simply spending quiet time alone can help us reconnect with our inner selves and reduce stress. By prioritizing our mental health, we cultivate emotional resilience and a sense of inner peace, allowing us to show up as our best selves in all areas of life.

Physical self-care is equally important, as our bodies are the vessels that carry us through life. Nourishing our bodies with proper nutrition, regular exercise, and adequate rest is an act of love that keeps us strong and energized. When we treat our bodies with care—

by engaging in activities we enjoy, eating foods that fuel us, and ensuring we get enough sleep—we send a powerful message to ourselves that we are worthy of care and attention. Simple habits like stretching in the morning, staying hydrated, and practicing deep breathing can have profound effects on both physical and mental health. By caring for our bodies, we show gratitude for the life we have and the experiences we get to enjoy.

Self-care also means engaging in activities that bring joy and fulfillment. Often, we get caught up in daily responsibilities, neglecting hobbies and passions that make us happy. Taking time to do what we love—whether it's reading, painting, dancing, traveling, or simply watching a favorite show—rejuvenates the soul and reminds us that life is meant to be enjoyed. Self-care is about listening to our hearts, honoring our desires, and allowing ourselves moments of pleasure without guilt. Love is not just about doing things for others; it is also about making sure we are happy, balanced, and fulfilled.

Ultimately, self-care is a continuous practice of honoring our needs, protecting our energy, and treating ourselves with kindness. It is not just about bubble baths or spa days, but about the everyday choices we make to support our well-being. By making self-care a priority, we affirm that we are valuable, deserving, and worthy of the same love that we so freely give to others. When we take care of ourselves, we not only enhance our own lives but also create deeper, more meaningful connections with the world around us.

Building Confidence Through Self-Compassion

Confidence is often seen as the ability to be bold, fearless, and self-assured, but at its core, true confidence comes from self-compassion. Many people believe that being confident means having no doubts or weaknesses, but in reality, confidence is built when we learn to embrace our imperfections with kindness and understanding. Self-compassion allows us to treat ourselves with the same patience and encouragement that we would offer to a loved one. When we practice self-compassion, we stop seeking validation from others and begin to trust in our own worth, leading to unshakable confidence that is rooted in self-acceptance rather than external approval.

One of the most important aspects of self-compassion is changing the way we talk to ourselves. Many people struggle with negative self-talk, often criticizing themselves for mistakes, flaws, or perceived shortcomings. These internal dialogues can damage self-esteem and make us feel unworthy of success or happiness. However, self-compassion teaches us to replace harsh self-criticism with kindness. Instead of saying, "I'm not good enough," we can say, "I am doing my best, and that is enough." By treating ourselves with the same gentleness and encouragement we would offer a friend, we begin to shift our mindset and develop a sense of confidence that is based on self-love rather than perfection.

Another powerful way to build confidence through self-compassion is embracing failure as a learning experience. Many people fear failure because they see it as a sign of inadequacy. However, failure is not a reflection of our worth—it is simply a part of growth. When we make mistakes, we have two choices: to criticize ourselves harshly or to recognize that setbacks are an opportunity to learn and improve. Self-compassion allows us to acknowledge our struggles without feeling ashamed. It reminds us that everyone faces challenges, and our value is not determined by how many times we fall but by how many times we rise. Confidence grows when we understand that mistakes do not define us; they guide us toward wisdom and strength.

Additionally, setting realistic expectations and celebrating progress is an essential part of self-compassion. Many people set impossibly high standards for themselves, believing they must be perfect in order to be confident. However, true confidence comes from acknowledging our progress, no matter how small. Every step forward—whether in personal growth, career, or relationships—is a sign of strength. By celebrating small victories, we reinforce the belief that we are capable and worthy. Confidence is not about achieving perfection; it is about recognizing our growth and being proud of the journey.

Ultimately, self-compassion is the foundation of lasting confidence. It allows us to accept ourselves fully, without the need for approval from others. When we treat ourselves with kindness, embrace our mistakes as lessons, and acknowledge our progress, we build a confidence that is resilient and enduring. Self-love and confidence go hand in hand—when we nurture one, the other naturally follows. By practicing self-compassion, we empower ourselves to step into the world with courage, knowing that our worth is not defined by external validation but by the love and kindness we show ourselves every day.

Chapter 11
Love Through Time – Keeping the Spark Alive

Love, in its early stages, is often filled with excitement, passion, and the thrill of discovery. However, as time passes, relationships evolve, and the initial spark that once ignited intense emotions may begin to fade. This does not mean love disappears; rather, it transforms into something deeper and more meaningful. Keeping the spark alive in a long-term relationship requires effort, intention, and a willingness to nurture the connection. Love is not just about falling for someone—it is about choosing them every day, even when the excitement of newness fades.

As relationships mature, partners often become comfortable with each other, which can sometimes lead to routine replacing romance. While comfort and security are essential, maintaining passion and excitement is equally important. Keeping love alive means making space for romance, adventure, and new experiences together. It involves continuing to date each other, finding joy in the little moments, and making an effort to express love in meaningful ways. Love flourishes when both partners actively seek ways to grow together, explore new aspects of their relationship, and cherish the bond they share.

The secret to lasting love is understanding that relationships require continuous investment. Passion does not fade because of time alone—it fades when partners stop making an effort to connect.

Communication, appreciation, and shared experiences are key to keeping love vibrant and fulfilling. Whether through small gestures, deep conversations, or finding new adventures to embark on together, maintaining the spark in a relationship is about choosing to keep love alive. True love is not just about how it begins but about how it is nurtured over time, ensuring that the bond grows stronger with each passing day.

Rekindling Passion in Long-Term Relationships

Passion is one of the key elements that keep a relationship exciting, fulfilling, and deeply connected. In the early stages of love, passion comes naturally—it is fueled by novelty, excitement, and the joy of discovering each other. However, as relationships mature and routine sets in, passion can sometimes fade. This does not mean that love is lost; it simply means that the fire needs to be rekindled. Passion is not something that automatically sustains itself; it requires effort, intentionality, and a willingness to continue nurturing the connection between two people.

One of the most effective ways to bring back passion is to prioritize quality time together. In long-term relationships, daily responsibilities such as work, family obligations, and personal commitments can take precedence, leaving little time for romance. Couples must make an effort to spend intentional, uninterrupted time together. Whether it is scheduling regular date nights, going on spontaneous trips, or simply setting aside time each day to connect without distractions, these moments help maintain emotional and physical intimacy. Shared experiences create new memories, reignite attraction, and remind partners why they fell in love in the first place.

Another important factor in rekindling passion is keeping the element of surprise alive. Routine can often make relationships feel predictable, which can lead to a decrease in excitement. Adding small surprises—such as unexpected love notes, thoughtful gestures, or planning a surprise getaway—can bring back a sense of anticipation and excitement. Even small changes, like trying a new activity together or experimenting with different ways to express affection, can reignite passion. The key is to break out of monotony and remind each other that love should be fun, exciting, and full of adventure.

Physical intimacy plays a crucial role in maintaining passion, but it is about more than just physical closeness—it is about deep emotional connection. Simple gestures such as holding hands, hugging, making eye contact, and engaging in affectionate touch throughout the day can help rekindle desire. Expressing love through physical touch releases oxytocin, the "bonding hormone," which strengthens emotional attachment and deepens intimacy. Couples should also prioritize open communication about their needs, desires, and ways to make their romantic connection stronger. When both partners feel emotionally and physically fulfilled, passion naturally returns to the relationship.

Lastly, one of the most overlooked ways to reignite passion is personal growth and self-care. When individuals focus on their own well-being, confidence, and personal development, they bring renewed energy into the relationship. Pursuing new hobbies, setting personal goals, and maintaining a sense of individuality can make partners more attractive to each other. Passion is not just about loving another person; it is also about maintaining a strong sense of self, which ultimately enhances the relationship.

Rekindling passion in a long-term relationship is not about trying to recreate the early days of love—it is about deepening the connection in a way that is fulfilling and sustainable. Love evolves, and so must the ways in which couples nurture it. By prioritizing time together, keeping romance alive, embracing physical intimacy, and fostering personal growth, passion can not only be reignited but can grow stronger with time. True passion is not fleeting; it is built and sustained through effort, appreciation, and a shared commitment to keeping love alive.

Growing Together Through Life's Changes

Change is an inevitable part of life. As individuals, we grow, evolve, and adapt to new circumstances, whether through career shifts, personal development, family changes, or unexpected life challenges. In a long-term relationship, growth does not happen in isolation; both partners must navigate these changes together. A strong, lasting love is not about avoiding change but about embracing it and finding ways to grow side by side. When a couple commits to evolving together rather than drifting apart, they build a foundation of resilience, adaptability, and deeper connection.

One of the most important aspects of growing together is open communication and understanding. Change can bring uncertainty, stress, or even fear, but talking openly about feelings, goals, and concerns helps strengthen the bond between partners. Whether it's discussing career aspirations, shifting family dynamics, or personal growth journeys, maintaining honest and supportive conversations ensures that both partners remain connected. When couples communicate effectively, they can navigate change as a team rather than facing it alone. Instead of resisting each other's transformations, they can embrace them and find ways to support one another's evolving dreams and ambitions.

Another key factor in growing together is learning to adapt and embrace new experiences. No two people remain the same throughout a relationship—priorities shift, perspectives change, and life circumstances evolve. Instead of fearing these changes, couples can view them as opportunities to deepen their connection. For example, transitioning into parenthood, relocating for a job, or adjusting to a new phase of life can either create distance or bring a couple closer, depending on their mindset. When partners actively choose to grow together—by supporting each other's ambitions, adjusting to new routines, and making an effort to stay connected—they create a love that is flexible and enduring.

A crucial part of growing together is also maintaining individual growth while nurturing the relationship. While it is essential to grow as a couple, it is equally important for each person to continue their personal journey. Pursuing passions, learning new skills, and developing as individuals enriches the relationship rather than detracts from it. When each partner is fulfilled on a personal level, they bring more energy, joy, and depth into their connection. Encouraging one another's growth—whether it's through education, career advancements, or self-improvement—creates a dynamic where both individuals thrive, making the relationship even stronger.

Finally, fostering patience, empathy, and mutual support is essential for navigating change together. Not all changes are easy, and some may bring challenges that test a relationship's strength. However, when couples choose to face life's uncertainties hand in hand, offering patience and understanding instead of resistance, they reinforce their commitment to each other. It is in the moments of uncertainty and transition that love is truly tested—and when navigated with care, it can deepen beyond measure.

Growing together through life's changes is about embracing the journey with an open heart, adapting to new realities, and choosing love even when things shift. When partners remain committed to evolving side by side, they create a relationship that is not only resilient but also fulfilling, ever-deepening, and built to withstand the test of time.

The Power of Shared Dreams

A strong and lasting relationship is built on more than just love and affection—it thrives on shared dreams, mutual goals, and a vision for the future. When two people align their aspirations and work toward common objectives, their bond deepens, and their connection strengthens. Shared dreams provide direction, inspire growth, and create a sense of unity that makes relationships more fulfilling. Whether it's building a life together, pursuing career ambitions, or embarking on new adventures, the power of shared dreams lies in the ability to inspire, motivate, and support each other through life's journey.

One of the greatest benefits of sharing dreams in a relationship is the sense of purpose and direction it provides. When couples discuss their hopes for the future—whether it's starting a family, traveling the world, or building a business together—they create a shared vision that strengthens their bond. Having mutual goals allows both partners to feel like they are working toward something meaningful, fostering teamwork and cooperation. Even in challenging times, having a common purpose can serve as a guiding light, reminding partners of what they are striving for together.

Beyond setting goals, shared dreams also strengthen emotional connection and trust. When partners openly discuss their aspirations, they become more vulnerable with each other, allowing deeper emotional intimacy to develop. Supporting each other's dreams requires trust—believing that your partner will stand by you, encourage you, and help you achieve your goals. This level of trust builds security in the relationship, ensuring that both individuals feel valued, heard, and understood. The act of dreaming together strengthens commitment, as it signifies a desire to build a future side by side rather than as separate individuals.

Another powerful aspect of shared dreams is the motivation and encouragement they bring. Pursuing goals can be daunting, but having a supportive partner makes the journey easier and more rewarding. Whether it's cheering each other on, providing constructive feedback, or celebrating small victories, shared dreams allow couples to uplift and inspire one another. When one partner feels discouraged, the other serves as a source of motivation, pushing them to keep going. This mutual support system fosters resilience, helping both partners overcome obstacles and turn their dreams into reality.

However, it is also important to recognize that shared dreams do not mean sacrificing individuality. Balancing personal aspirations with mutual goals is key to a healthy and thriving relationship. Each person should have space to pursue their own passions while also contributing to the shared vision they have as a couple. Encouraging each other's personal growth while working toward common dreams ensures that both individuals feel fulfilled in their own right while also strengthening their relationship.

Ultimately, the power of shared dreams lies in the bond they create, the trust they reinforce, and the excitement they bring to a relationship. They remind couples that love is not just about the present—it is about building a future together, hand in hand. When two people dream together, they not only create a vision for their lives but also build a foundation of love, support, and commitment that grows stronger with time.

Chapter 12
The Language of Love – Understanding Emotional Expression

Love is a universal emotion, but the way it is expressed and understood can vary from person to person. Just as different languages exist in the world, love also has its own unique ways of communication. Some people express love through words, while others show it through actions, touch, or time spent together. Understanding these different expressions of love is crucial in building strong and meaningful relationships. When partners, friends, or family members learn to recognize and appreciate each other's emotional expressions, they foster deeper connections and greater harmony in their relationships.

The concept of love languages helps explain why people express and receive love differently. Some individuals feel most loved when they hear words of affirmation, while others find love in acts of service, physical touch, receiving gifts, or quality time. When these expressions do not align, misunderstandings can arise, leading to feelings of neglect or frustration. For example, one partner may constantly say "I love you," while the other may prefer love to be demonstrated through actions rather than words. Learning to speak and understand each other's love language helps bridge these gaps, ensuring that love is felt in the way it is meant to be received.

Beyond love languages, emotional expression in relationships requires open communication and emotional intelligence. People often struggle to express their feelings due to fear, past experiences, or differences in upbringing. However, being able to communicate emotions honestly and listen with empathy strengthens trust and intimacy. When love is expressed in ways that resonate with both partners, it creates a deep and lasting bond. By understanding the different ways love is communicated and making an effort to express it in meaningful ways, relationships become more fulfilling, supportive, and enduring.

Love Languages and Their Impact

Love is a powerful force that connects people, but not everyone expresses or receives love in the same way. The concept of love languages, introduced by Dr. Gary Chapman, explains that individuals have different ways of giving and receiving love. Understanding these love languages can transform relationships by ensuring that love is communicated in a way that resonates with both partners. When people express love in ways that align with their partner's needs, relationships become stronger, more fulfilling, and more deeply connected.

There are five primary love languages: words of affirmation, acts of service, receiving gifts, quality time, and physical touch. Each love language represents a different way in which people feel most valued and appreciated. Words of affirmation involve verbal expressions of love, such as compliments, encouragement, and affectionate words. For individuals who value this love language, a heartfelt "I love you" or words of appreciation can mean the world. On the other hand, acts of service focus on actions rather than words—doing something helpful for a loved one, like preparing a meal, handling a responsibility, or offering support during a stressful time.

Receiving gifts is another love language, where thoughtful presents symbolize love and appreciation. It is not about materialism but rather about the effort and thought behind the gesture. A well-chosen gift, even something small, can serve as a lasting reminder of love. Meanwhile, quality time is about giving undivided attention and prioritizing shared experiences. People who favor this love language feel most loved when they engage in meaningful conversations, spend uninterrupted time together, or share special activities. Lastly, physical touch involves affectionate gestures such as hugs, hand-holding, or gentle touches. For those who value physical connection, a warm embrace or a reassuring touch can be the most powerful expression of love.

Recognizing and understanding love languages can have a profound impact on relationships. Often, people naturally express love in the way they prefer to receive it, but this may not always align with their partner's needs. For instance, someone who expresses love through acts of service may not realize that their partner craves words of affirmation instead. This mismatch can lead to misunderstandings, frustration, and feelings of being unloved or unappreciated. However, when individuals take the time to understand and adapt to each other's love languages, they create a more harmonious and emotionally fulfilling relationship.

Beyond romantic relationships, love languages also apply to friendships, family bonds, and even workplace connections. Expressing love and appreciation in the right way strengthens emotional ties, reduces conflict, and fosters deeper trust. Parents who understand their children's love languages can nurture them in ways that make them feel truly valued. Friends who recognize each other's needs can support one another more effectively. Even in professional environments, acknowledging different forms of appreciation can enhance teamwork and morale.

Ultimately, love languages serve as a bridge to deeper emotional understanding and connection. When love is expressed in a way that truly speaks to someone's heart, it reinforces the bond and strengthens the foundation of any relationship. By learning to identify and honor the love languages of those around us, we create relationships that are not only loving but also deeply fulfilling and lasting.

The Art of Listening in Relationships

Communication is the foundation of any healthy relationship, but true connection is built not just through words, but through listening. The art of listening goes beyond simply hearing what someone says—it involves fully engaging, understanding, and responding in a way that makes the other person feel valued and respected. When people actively listen to one another, they create a deeper emotional bond, reduce misunderstandings, and strengthen trust. In relationships, listening is one of the most powerful ways to show love, care, and empathy.

One of the biggest challenges in communication is that many people listen to respond rather than to understand. Instead of focusing on the speaker's words, they may be thinking about what they will say next, forming counterarguments, or getting distracted by their own emotions. This can lead to misunderstandings, frustration, and feelings of being unheard. Active listening, on the other hand, requires patience and full attention. It means putting aside distractions, maintaining eye contact, and truly absorbing what the other person is expressing. When partners feel heard, they are more likely to open up, share their feelings, and feel safe in the relationship.

Another key aspect of the art of listening is empathy and emotional validation. People do not always seek advice or solutions; sometimes, they just need to feel understood. A partner who listens with empathy acknowledges emotions without judgment. Simple phrases like "I understand how you feel," "That sounds really tough," or "I appreciate you sharing this with me" can make a huge difference. Emotional validation reassures the other person that their feelings are seen and respected, strengthening the emotional connection between partners.

Nonverbal communication also plays a crucial role in listening. Body language, facial expressions, and tone of voice all contribute to how well a person is perceived as listening. Nodding, maintaining an open posture, and responding with appropriate expressions help convey attentiveness. Small affirmations like "I see," "That makes sense," or even a simple touch on the hand can enhance communication and make the speaker feel more comfortable expressing their thoughts. Being aware of one's own body language and reactions is just as important as the words spoken.

Listening also requires patience and the ability to handle difficult conversations. Not all discussions are easy, and emotions can sometimes run high. It is important to remain calm, avoid interrupting, and allow the speaker to finish their thoughts before responding. Even if there is disagreement, listening with an open mind can prevent arguments from escalating and pave the way for constructive conversations. Instead of dismissing the other person's perspective, asking clarifying questions like "Can you tell me more about how you feel?" can foster deeper understanding.

Ultimately, the art of listening strengthens relationships by fostering trust, intimacy, and emotional security. When people feel heard, they feel valued. When partners make a habit of truly listening to each other, they create a safe and loving space where both voices matter. Whether in romantic relationships, friendships, or family bonds, being a good listener is one of the most meaningful ways to show love and support.

Expressing Love in Words and Actions

Love is a powerful emotion, but it becomes meaningful only when it is expressed in ways that can be felt and understood. Some people express love through words, while others show it through their actions. Both are essential in building strong relationships, as love that is spoken but not shown may feel empty, while love that is acted upon but never verbalized can sometimes leave doubts. True love flourishes when words and actions align, reinforcing emotional connection and deepening the bond between partners, friends, and family.

Words hold immense power in expressing love. Simple phrases like "I love you," "I appreciate you," and "You mean the world to me" can make a significant impact on a person's emotions. Compliments, affirmations, and heartfelt conversations help people feel valued and understood. However, love is not just about saying the right things; it is about speaking with sincerity. Thoughtful words, when spoken genuinely, can bring comfort, reassurance, and joy. In relationships, open communication fosters deeper intimacy. Expressing love verbally is especially important for those who value words of affirmation, as hearing affectionate words regularly strengthens their sense of connection and security.

However, love cannot rely on words alone—it must also be demonstrated through actions. Actions prove love in ways that words cannot. Small daily gestures, such as making a loved one's favorite meal, remembering important dates, or offering help when they need it, show thoughtfulness and care. Love in action is about being present—listening when they speak, supporting them through difficulties, and showing up when it matters most. These everyday expressions of love reinforce emotional bonds and make relationships stronger. A person who loves deeply will not just say they care; they will prove it through their behavior and consistent effort.

One of the most profound ways to express love through actions is by prioritizing quality time. In the digital age, distractions often pull people away from meaningful interactions. However, love grows when time is intentionally set aside for deep conversations, shared experiences, and making memories together. Whether it is planning a special date, taking a walk together, or simply sitting in silence while holding hands, quality time allows partners, friends, and family members to feel connected. It sends the message that their presence is valued and that their relationship is worth investing in.

Additionally, love is expressed through physical touch and acts of service. A warm hug, a reassuring touch, or holding hands can provide comfort, security, and a sense of closeness. For those who value physical affection, these small gestures communicate love without the need for words. Similarly, acts of service—doing something meaningful for a loved one, even if it is as simple as running an errand or helping with a task—show dedication and care.

These thoughtful actions demonstrate selflessness and a willingness to contribute to their happiness.

Ultimately, love is best expressed when words and actions align. Saying "I love you" while consistently showing care and effort creates a relationship built on trust, appreciation, and emotional security. Whether spoken or demonstrated, love should be a daily practice — one that nurtures, uplifts, and strengthens the bond between two hearts.

Chapter 13
A Legacy of Love – Creating Meaningful Connections

Love is not just about the moments we share in the present—it is about the impact we leave behind, the connections we nurture, and the way we inspire others through our actions. A legacy of love is built through the relationships we cultivate, the kindness we extend, and the values we pass down. It is not measured by material possessions or grand achievements but by the way we touch the lives of others, leaving a lasting impression of warmth, care, and understanding. Creating meaningful connections ensures that our love continues to live on, even beyond our presence, shaping the hearts and lives of those around us.

Meaningful connections are formed through genuine presence, deep empathy, and consistent effort. Love that is enduring is not fleeting or conditional—it is rooted in trust, compassion, and a willingness to show up, even in difficult times. Whether it is through family, friendships, or community, the relationships we nurture shape the world we live in. By investing in authentic, heartfelt connections, we create a space where love is felt, remembered, and carried forward by those we have touched. These bonds are what give life meaning, providing a sense of belonging and purpose that outlasts temporary hardships.

Leaving a legacy of love also means leading by example and inspiring others to love deeply and authentically. When we practice kindness, forgiveness, and generosity, we encourage those around us to do the same. Love, when given freely, has a ripple effect—it spreads beyond individual relationships and fosters a culture of warmth, understanding, and acceptance. Whether through small everyday gestures or profound lifelong commitments, the love we share leaves an imprint, shaping future generations and ensuring that our legacy is not just one of existence, but of true, heartfelt connection.

Love That Inspires Generations

Love is one of the most powerful forces that can be passed down through generations, shaping the values, beliefs, and emotional well-being of those who come after us. Whether through the love of parents for their children, the bond between siblings, or the kindness extended within a community, love has the ability to create a lasting legacy. When love is demonstrated with sincerity, patience, and care, it becomes a guiding light, inspiring future generations to build strong, meaningful relationships. The way we express love today has a profound impact on how love is understood and practiced in the future.

One of the most significant ways love is passed down is through family relationships and traditions. The love shown by parents, grandparents, and caregivers serves as the first example of emotional connection for children. A nurturing, affectionate environment teaches children the importance of kindness, respect, and empathy. When children grow up witnessing love expressed through thoughtful gestures, supportive words, and unwavering presence, they learn to carry those same values into their own relationships. A loving home sets the foundation for emotional security, allowing individuals to develop healthy attachments and a deep appreciation for the power of love.

Beyond family, love that inspires generations is also found in stories, wisdom, and acts of kindness that endure over time. Love is not just an emotion but a way of life, reflected in the lessons passed down from elders to younger generations. Whether through heartfelt advice, shared experiences, or the lessons of perseverance and resilience, love is a guiding force that teaches people how to navigate life's challenges with grace. Grandparents sharing stories of enduring love, parents demonstrating patience and sacrifice, and mentors encouraging personal growth all contribute to shaping a generation that understands the true depth of love.

Additionally, love that inspires future generations is built through acts of kindness and compassion beyond personal relationships. A person's legacy of love is not only measured by how they treat their family but also by how they impact their community and the world around them. Small acts of kindness, such as helping a stranger, supporting a cause, or standing up for those in need, create ripples of love that extend far beyond immediate relationships. When children and young people see love in action—through generosity, forgiveness, and selflessness—they are encouraged to continue spreading love in their own ways.

Ultimately, love that inspires generations is about leading by example and choosing love as a lifelong commitment. The way we express love today influences how future generations understand relationships, empathy, and human connection. By showing love in both big and small ways—through presence, words, and actions—we create a legacy that lasts beyond our lifetime. Love is not just a fleeting feeling; it is a force that can shape families, communities, and even the world when nurtured with care and intention. In the end, the greatest gift we can leave behind is a legacy of love that continues to inspire, heal, and bring people together for generations to come.

Acts of Kindness That Spread Love

Love is often thought of as an emotion shared between partners, family members, or close friends, but its true power lies in its ability to extend beyond personal relationships and reach the wider world. Acts of kindness are one of the simplest yet most profound ways to spread love. A small gesture, a kind word, or an act of generosity can create ripples that touch lives in unexpected and beautiful ways. When we choose kindness, we not only brighten someone's day but also contribute to a culture of love, empathy, and compassion that extends far beyond our immediate circle.

One of the most powerful aspects of kindness is its ability to create deep emotional impact with minimal effort. A simple smile, a heartfelt compliment, or a helping hand can make a significant difference in someone's life. Often, people are struggling with difficulties that are not visible to others, and a single act of kindness can provide comfort and reassurance. Whether it is paying for someone's coffee, holding the door open, or offering a listening ear to a friend in need, these small gestures reinforce the idea that love is not only found in grand romantic expressions but in everyday moments of care and consideration.

Beyond small gestures, acts of service and generosity create lasting bonds and foster a sense of community. Volunteering at a shelter, donating to a cause, or mentoring someone in need are ways to spread love in a more impactful manner. These actions go beyond momentary kindness—they create sustainable change and inspire others to do the same. When people witness acts of kindness, they are more likely to pass them on, creating a ripple effect that continues to grow. The love we put into the world through selfless actions often returns in unexpected ways, reinforcing the idea that kindness is a cycle that nourishes both the giver and the receiver.

Another significant way to spread love through kindness is by showing empathy and compassion in our daily interactions. In a world where people are often quick to judge or react, choosing patience, understanding, and forgiveness can be transformative. Being kind does not always mean grand gestures; sometimes, it means giving someone the benefit of the doubt, listening without interrupting, or offering words of encouragement when someone feels defeated. True kindness requires us to see beyond our own experiences and acknowledge the struggles, hopes, and humanity of those around us.

Finally, acts of kindness remind us that love is not limited to personal relationships but is a universal language that connects us all. Every small act of love contributes to a larger movement of compassion, creating a world where people feel valued and supported. Whether through words, actions, or silent gestures of goodwill, kindness has the power to heal wounds, bridge divides, and remind us of our shared humanity. By choosing to spread love through kindness, we contribute to a world where love is not just a fleeting emotion but a force that binds us all together.

Leaving a Legacy of Compassion and Care

A true legacy is not measured by wealth, fame, or accomplishments but by the impact one leaves on the lives of others. A legacy of compassion and care is built through kindness, empathy, and the love shared with family, friends, and even strangers. It is about making the world a better place—not just for oneself but for future generations. When we live with compassion, we create a lasting ripple effect, inspiring others to act with kindness and fostering a culture of love that transcends time.

One of the most meaningful ways to leave a legacy of compassion is by leading with kindness in our daily interactions. Whether through small gestures like offering words of encouragement, being patient in difficult situations, or actively listening to those in need, acts of kindness create a profound impact. Many people remember how they were treated far more than the specific words spoken to them. By treating others with respect, understanding, and love, we create memories that endure, shaping how people perceive love and human connection.

Beyond individual interactions, a legacy of care can be established through service and acts of generosity. Volunteering, mentoring, supporting charitable causes, or simply offering a helping hand to those who need it are all ways to spread love beyond personal relationships. When we dedicate time to uplifting others, we create an environment where love and kindness become contagious. Teaching children, friends, and communities the value of generosity ensures that the principles of care and compassion continue beyond our lifetime. The impact of such actions is often greater than we realize—something as simple as encouraging a struggling friend or donating to a cause can set off a chain reaction of goodwill.

A lasting legacy is also built through the values and lessons we pass down to others. Parents, mentors, and community leaders have a unique opportunity to shape future generations by demonstrating the power of love, respect, and selflessness. Teaching children the importance of empathy, showing them how to care for others, and encouraging them to embrace diversity and understanding ensures that compassion continues to thrive. Through storytelling, personal examples, and intentional acts of love, we create a world where kindness becomes an ingrained value, not just an occasional act.

Finally, leaving a legacy of compassion and care means being remembered for the love we shared and the positive impact we made. When people think back on their interactions with us, they will not remember the material things we owned but the warmth, encouragement, and kindness we extended. True success in life is not about what we take but what we give. A compassionate heart leaves behind a legacy that continues to touch lives long after we are gone, proving that love and care are the most enduring gifts we can offer.

Ultimately, a legacy of compassion and care is about making love a lifelong practice. It is about choosing kindness, spreading joy, and leaving behind a world that is just a little bit better because of the love we contributed. By living with empathy and selflessness, we create a legacy that outlives us, inspiring future generations to walk the same path of love and kindness.

Chapter 14
The Healing Power of Love – Overcoming Pain and Heartbreak

Love is often seen as a source of joy, connection, and fulfillment, but it is also deeply intertwined with pain and heartbreak. Every person who experiences love must, at some point, confront loss, disappointment, or emotional wounds. Whether it is the end of a relationship, the loss of a loved one, or the betrayal of trust, heartbreak can feel overwhelming. Yet, love itself holds the power to heal. While heartbreak may leave scars, love—whether from within, from others, or from new beginnings—has the capacity to mend, restore, and strengthen the human heart.

Healing through love does not mean forgetting pain or suppressing emotions; rather, it means allowing love to be a source of comfort, growth, and renewal. In times of loss, the love of friends, family, and even self-love can provide the strength needed to move forward. Love helps us to see beyond the pain, to find meaning in difficult experiences, and to remind us that we are not alone. It is through love that we learn resilience, allowing past wounds to transform us instead of breaking us.

Overcoming heartbreak is a journey—one that requires patience, self-compassion, and a willingness to embrace love again. The heart, though fragile, is incredibly resilient. It can heal, open again, and even love more deeply after experiencing pain. Whether through self-reflection, supportive relationships, or new experiences, love continues to guide us toward healing. By understanding the power of love to overcome pain, we learn that even in our darkest moments, love remains a light that leads us back to wholeness.

Love as a Source of Emotional Healing

Love has an extraordinary ability to heal emotional wounds, offering comfort, strength, and renewal in times of pain. Whether through the love of family, friends, or even self-love, genuine emotional connection has the power to mend broken hearts and restore hope. When we experience loss, betrayal, or heartbreak, it is love that helps us rebuild, giving us the courage to move forward. Healing does not mean erasing pain, but rather learning how to carry it with grace, using love as a guiding force to find peace and renewal.

One of the most profound ways love heals is through the power of presence and support. When we face emotional struggles, having someone who genuinely listens, understands, and offers reassurance can make a world of difference. A hug from a loved one, a comforting conversation, or simply the feeling of not being alone can bring immense relief. Emotional healing often begins when we feel seen and valued, and love—whether from a partner, a close friend, or a caring family member—creates a safe space for us to process our pain. Love does not always come in grand gestures; sometimes, the quiet presence of someone who truly cares is enough to ease our burdens.

Beyond external support, self-love is an essential part of emotional healing. Often, people seek validation and comfort from others, forgetting that true healing must also come from within. Learning to love oneself, despite past pain and imperfections, is a transformative process. Practicing self-care, engaging in positive self-talk, and forgiving oneself for past mistakes can gradually restore self-worth. Love teaches us that we are worthy of happiness, even after experiencing deep emotional wounds. By embracing self-love, we build resilience, allowing ourselves to move beyond pain and step into a place of growth and renewal.

Another way love heals is through forgiveness and letting go. Holding onto resentment or anger after being hurt can prolong emotional suffering. Love, however, teaches us the value of forgiveness—not necessarily for the other person, but for ourselves. Letting go of pain does not mean forgetting what happened or justifying it; it means releasing the weight of negativity so that we can heal. Love allows us to choose peace over bitterness, understanding that healing comes from freeing ourselves from emotional burdens. Whether it is forgiving someone else or forgiving ourselves, love leads to a sense of closure and emotional freedom.

Lastly, love provides hope for new beginnings. Even after heartbreak, loss, or trauma, love continues to exist in many forms. A failed relationship does not mean love is gone forever, and a painful experience does not mean happiness is unattainable. Love has a way of finding us again—through new friendships, fresh opportunities, or even through personal growth. It reminds us that pain is temporary, but the capacity to love and be loved is infinite.

In the end, love is one of the most powerful sources of emotional healing. It does not erase pain but helps us navigate it with strength and grace. Whether through human connection, self-compassion, or the ability to forgive and move forward, love teaches us that even after the deepest wounds, healing is always possible.

Finding Strength in Love After Loss

Loss is one of the most painful experiences in life, whether it is the loss of a loved one, a relationship, or a dream that once felt certain. Grief can be overwhelming, leaving a void that seems impossible to fill. However, even in the midst of loss, love remains. Love does not disappear with loss; instead, it transforms, offering strength, healing, and resilience. Finding strength in love after loss is not about forgetting or moving on too quickly—it is about allowing love to guide us through pain, helping us rebuild our hearts and find meaning again.

One of the most profound ways love provides strength after loss is through the memories and lessons it leaves behind. The love shared with someone does not vanish when they are no longer physically present. Instead, it lives on in the cherished moments, the wisdom imparted, and the impact they had on our lives. Whether it is a loved one who has passed away or a relationship that has ended, love continues to shape who we are. Remembering the joy, support, and kindness experienced in that love allows us to carry a part of it forward, finding comfort in knowing that love, once given, is never truly lost.

Another source of strength comes from the love and support of those who remain. In times of grief, it is easy to feel isolated, believing that no one can fully understand the pain we are experiencing. However, love is not limited to a single person or relationship. Friends, family, and even compassionate strangers can offer support, reminding us that we are not alone. Allowing ourselves to lean on others during difficult times helps in the healing process. Love exists in many forms, and when one source of love is lost, others can step in to provide comfort, reassurance, and a sense of belonging.

Self-love and personal growth are also crucial in finding strength after loss. It is natural to feel broken, lost, or unworthy after experiencing deep sorrow. However, loss does not define a person—how they rise from it does. Practicing self-care, acknowledging emotions, and giving oneself permission to heal are acts of love that foster resilience. Engaging in activities that bring joy, rediscovering passions, and setting new goals help shift focus from pain to renewal. Loss, as devastating as it may be, can also be an opportunity for transformation and self-discovery.

Lastly, love provides the courage to open one's heart again. After experiencing loss, it can be difficult to trust, to hope, or to love again. The fear of more pain can be paralyzing. However, love is not meant to be feared; it is meant to be embraced. The ability to love again—whether in the form of new relationships, friendships, or self-acceptance—is a testament to the human heart's resilience. Love teaches that even after immense pain, life still holds moments of joy, connection, and purpose.

Finding strength in love after loss is not about forgetting, but about allowing love to be a source of healing. It is about carrying forward the love that was shared, seeking support from those who care, nurturing oneself, and finding the courage to love again. Even in the face of heartbreak, love remains the most powerful force that allows us to heal, grow, and rediscover the beauty of life.

Turning Pain into Growth Through Love

Pain is an inevitable part of life, often caused by heartbreak, loss, betrayal, or disappointment. While suffering can feel overwhelming, it also presents an opportunity for transformation. Love, in its many forms—whether self-love, the love of others, or the love we cultivate for life itself—has the power to turn pain into growth. When we embrace love as a guiding force, we shift our perspective, heal our wounds, and emerge stronger, wiser, and more resilient. Growth through love does not mean ignoring pain but rather learning from it and using it as a stepping stone toward a more fulfilling life.

One of the most powerful ways love transforms pain is through self-compassion and acceptance. When we experience loss or hardship, our first instinct may be to blame ourselves, dwell on past mistakes, or struggle with feelings of unworthiness. However, love teaches us to treat ourselves with kindness, just as we would a dear friend. Instead of seeing pain as a punishment, we can view it as a part of our journey, allowing ourselves to feel, heal, and grow without judgment. Practicing self-love through self-care, positive affirmations, and personal forgiveness creates a nurturing environment where pain is not a burden but a lesson in resilience.

Another way love helps us grow through pain is by teaching us the importance of human connection. Heartbreak or loss may make us want to withdraw from others, fearing vulnerability or further disappointment. However, love reminds us that we are not alone. Seeking comfort in supportive relationships—whether through family, friends, or even new connections—can provide emotional healing and renewed strength. The kindness and understanding of others help us see that pain is temporary and that love, in its many forms, continues to surround us. True growth happens when we allow love to soften our pain instead of hardening our hearts.

Love also gives us the strength to redefine our perspective on pain. Instead of viewing challenges as setbacks, love encourages us to see them as opportunities for self-discovery and transformation. A failed relationship can teach us about our values, boundaries, and what we truly need in a partner. Personal loss can deepen our appreciation for the time we have and the people who remain. Betrayal can strengthen our ability to recognize true loyalty and honesty. Every painful experience carries a lesson, and love helps us extract wisdom from even the darkest moments. Growth happens when we embrace pain as a teacher rather than an enemy.

Ultimately, turning pain into growth through love is about choosing hope over despair. While we cannot always control what happens to us, we can control how we respond. Choosing love—whether by healing ourselves, reconnecting with others, or finding deeper meaning in life—allows us to rise from pain stronger than before. Love teaches us that no experience is wasted if it helps us grow, and even the deepest wounds can lead to the greatest transformation. In the end, love is not just what heals pain; it is what turns pain into the foundation of a more profound and purposeful life.

Chapter 15
Love in the Digital Age – Navigating Modern Relationships

In today's world, technology has transformed the way people connect, communicate, and express love. From texting and video calls to social media and dating apps, relationships are now shaped by digital interactions as much as by face-to-face connections. While technology has made it easier to stay in touch with loved ones across distances, it has also introduced new challenges. Navigating love in the digital age requires a balance between embracing technological advancements and maintaining genuine emotional intimacy. Modern relationships must adapt to these changes while ensuring that love remains personal, meaningful, and fulfilling.

One of the greatest benefits of digital communication is its ability to bring people closer, regardless of distance. Long-distance relationships are more manageable than ever, and online dating has expanded the possibilities of meeting new people. Social media allows couples to share their experiences, celebrate milestones, and express love in creative ways. However, the same digital tools that enhance connection can also create misunderstandings, unrealistic expectations, and even emotional distance. Over-reliance on technology can sometimes replace deep, meaningful conversations with quick texts or emojis, making it essential to find a balance between digital and real-world interactions.

Beyond communication, the digital age has also redefined expectations in relationships. The pressure to showcase a "perfect" love life on social media, the challenges of maintaining trust in an era of constant connectivity, and the blurred lines between online and offline relationships have added new complexities. Modern love requires intentionality—choosing quality time over screen time, setting healthy boundaries with social media, and prioritizing real emotional connections over digital validation. By navigating these challenges with awareness and open communication, couples can use technology as a tool to enhance love rather than replace it.

The Impact of Technology on Love and Communication

Technology has dramatically transformed the way people experience love and relationships, reshaping communication, intimacy, and expectations. While digital advancements have made it easier to connect, express affection, and maintain long-distance relationships, they have also introduced new challenges. The way we navigate love in the digital age depends on how we use technology—whether as a tool to strengthen connections or as a distraction that distances us from meaningful relationships. The key lies in balancing digital interactions with real-world emotional intimacy.

One of the most significant ways technology has impacted love is by bridging the gap between distance and time. Long-distance relationships, which were once difficult to sustain, have become more manageable thanks to instant messaging, video calls, and social media. Couples can now share daily experiences, communicate in real-time, and maintain emotional closeness despite physical separation. Online dating has also revolutionized the way people meet and form romantic relationships, expanding opportunities beyond geographical limitations. For many, technology has made love more accessible, allowing people to form deep connections that might not have been possible otherwise.

However, while technology enhances connection, it also has the potential to create emotional distance and misunderstandings. Digital communication, though convenient, lacks the depth of face-to-face interactions. Texting and messaging, for instance, can lead to misinterpretations, as tone and intent are not always clear. Emojis and short responses may replace meaningful conversations, making communication feel superficial. Additionally, the constant availability of messaging apps can sometimes create unrealistic expectations about instant replies, leading to unnecessary stress or misunderstandings in relationships.

Social media has also redefined the way love is expressed and perceived. Many couples use platforms like Instagram and Facebook to share moments of their relationship, celebrating love through posts, pictures, and public declarations. While this can be a positive way to express appreciation, it can also create pressure to maintain a "perfect" relationship online. Comparing one's relationship to idealized versions seen on social media can lead to dissatisfaction, insecurity, or even unnecessary conflict. Love should not be measured by likes or comments but by genuine emotional connection and trust.

Another challenge brought by technology is the blurred boundaries between personal space and digital presence. The constant accessibility of smartphones and social media can make it difficult for couples to be fully present with each other. Many relationships suffer when partners prioritize screens over meaningful face-to-face interactions. Moments that could be spent building deeper emotional intimacy are sometimes lost to mindless scrolling, online distractions, or digital dependencies. Setting boundaries—such as limiting phone use during dates or prioritizing quality conversations—can help couples maintain a stronger connection beyond their digital devices.

Ultimately, the impact of technology on love and communication depends on how it is used. When embraced mindfully, digital tools can strengthen relationships, enhance communication, and make love more accessible. However, over-reliance on technology without real emotional effort can weaken intimacy. Striking a balance between online and offline interactions, setting healthy digital boundaries, and prioritizing meaningful conversations ensure that technology serves love rather than replaces it. Love in the digital age requires awareness, intentionality, and a commitment to real connection beyond the screen.

Balancing Virtual and Real-World Connections

In the digital age, relationships are often influenced by both virtual and real-world interactions. While technology provides countless ways to stay connected, maintaining a healthy balance between digital communication and face-to-face interactions is essential for building meaningful relationships. Virtual connections—through texting, video calls, and social media—offer convenience and accessibility, but they should not replace the depth and authenticity of in-person relationships. Striking the right balance ensures that love and friendships remain strong, fulfilling, and rooted in genuine emotional connection.

One of the biggest advantages of virtual communication is its ability to keep relationships alive across distances. Whether it's maintaining a long-distance romantic relationship, staying in touch with family, or nurturing friendships across time zones, technology allows people to stay emotionally connected despite physical separation. Instant messaging and video calls help bridge the gap, making it easier to share daily moments, express emotions, and offer support. However, while these tools enhance communication, they should complement rather than replace in-person interactions whenever possible. Relying solely on digital connections can create a sense of detachment, as virtual interactions often lack the warmth and nonverbal cues present in face-to-face communication.

On the other hand, an over-dependence on digital interactions can sometimes lead to disconnection in real-life relationships. Many people find themselves glued to their screens even when sitting next to their loved ones, scrolling through social media instead of engaging in meaningful conversations. This can create emotional distance, as partners, friends, and family members may feel neglected or unimportant. Real-world connections thrive on presence—being physically and emotionally available during shared moments. Simple practices, such as setting phone-free dinner times or prioritizing face-to-face conversations, help reinforce the importance of genuine presence in relationships.

Another challenge in balancing virtual and real-world connections is managing expectations and boundaries. The constant accessibility of digital communication can sometimes lead to unrealistic expectations about immediate responses. In romantic relationships, for example, one partner may expect instant replies, leading to unnecessary stress and misunderstandings. Setting healthy boundaries—such as designating times to unplug from devices or having open discussions about communication preferences—helps prevent digital fatigue while fostering a sense of security in the relationship. Mutual understanding of online and offline availability ensures that technology remains a tool for connection rather than a source of pressure.

Maintaining a balance also means being intentional about quality time spent together in person. While virtual communication is convenient, nothing compares to shared experiences in the real world. Engaging in activities together—such as traveling, having meaningful conversations, enjoying meals, or even engaging in simple everyday moments—strengthens relationships in ways that digital interactions cannot. The emotional depth, physical presence, and spontaneous expressions of affection that come with face-to-face interactions are irreplaceable.

Ultimately, balancing virtual and real-world connections requires mindfulness and effort. Technology should be used to enhance relationships, not replace them. By prioritizing face-to-face interactions, setting healthy digital boundaries, and ensuring that love and friendships are nurtured beyond the screen, people can build relationships that are both technologically connected and deeply rooted in genuine emotional intimacy.

Maintaining Emotional Intimacy in a Digital World

In today's digital world, relationships are constantly shaped by technology. While instant messaging, video calls, and social media platforms provide new ways to stay connected, they can also pose challenges to emotional intimacy. True emotional closeness is built on trust, deep conversations, and meaningful interactions—things that cannot always be fully expressed through screens. To maintain emotional intimacy in a world dominated by digital communication, couples and loved ones must intentionally nurture their connection, ensuring that technology enhances rather than replaces genuine emotional bonds.

One of the key factors in maintaining emotional intimacy is prioritizing quality communication. Digital conversations often rely on quick texts, emojis, and short responses, which can sometimes lack depth and emotional nuance. While technology allows for instant communication, it is important to have meaningful conversations where both individuals feel heard and understood. Voice and video calls can bridge the gap between text-based messages and in-person interactions, but even these require effort. Asking thoughtful questions, actively listening, and expressing genuine emotions help keep digital conversations engaging and emotionally fulfilling.

Another essential aspect of maintaining intimacy is being present and emotionally available, even in digital spaces. In long-distance relationships or friendships, technology is often the primary mode of communication, making it essential to be emotionally invested in conversations. Instead of multitasking while texting or scrolling through social media during a video call, giving full attention to a conversation strengthens the connection. Emotional intimacy is not just about words; it is about making the other person feel valued, respected, and prioritized, regardless of whether the interaction is digital or in-person.

Trust and transparency also play a significant role in maintaining emotional closeness in a digital age. With social media and constant online activity, misunderstandings and insecurities can arise. Seeing a partner or friend engaging with others online while neglecting personal communication can lead to feelings of distance or exclusion. Open discussions about online boundaries, expectations, and digital habits help prevent unnecessary doubts and reinforce trust.

Transparency in digital interactions—such as sharing feelings, discussing concerns, and being honest about time spent online—ensures that emotional connection remains strong and secure.

In addition to communication and trust, intentional effort to create shared experiences can strengthen emotional intimacy. While physical distance or busy schedules might prevent in-person meetings, couples and loved ones can find creative ways to bond through technology. Watching movies together via streaming services, playing online games, sending thoughtful voice messages, or writing heartfelt emails can create a sense of closeness even when physically apart. These shared experiences help maintain the feeling of connection, making digital interactions more meaningful and engaging.

Ultimately, maintaining emotional intimacy in a digital world requires intentionality, effort, and a balance between online and offline connections. While technology offers convenience, real emotional closeness is built through deep conversations, trust, and shared moments that go beyond screens. By being present, communicating openly, and making time for meaningful interactions, relationships can thrive despite the digital age's challenges. When used wisely, technology can be a bridge rather than a barrier, helping love and emotional intimacy flourish in a modern world.

Chapter 16
Love and Destiny – The Role of Fate in Relationships

Love is often seen as a beautiful mystery, guided by forces beyond our control. Many people believe in the idea of destiny—that certain relationships are meant to be, and that some souls are destined to find each other. Whether it is through serendipitous encounters, shared dreams, or an unexplainable connection, fate is often credited for bringing two people together. While some see love as a matter of choice and effort, others believe that destiny plays a significant role in shaping relationships. The question remains: is love a product of fate, or do we create our own love stories through the decisions we make?

The concept of soulmates and meant-to-be relationships has existed across cultures for centuries. Stories of lovers brought together by destiny—whether through divine intervention, fate, or cosmic alignment—have long fascinated humanity. Some believe that certain people enter our lives for a reason, helping us grow, teaching us valuable lessons, or even staying with us forever. However, while fate may bring people together, it is ultimately up to them to nurture the love they find. A strong relationship is not just about meeting the right person at the right time; it is about choosing to build something meaningful every day.

Even if fate plays a role in love, relationships are sustained by effort, understanding, and commitment. While destiny may create the opportunity for love, it is human connection, shared experiences, and emotional investment that determine whether a relationship thrives. Love, in many ways, is a dance between fate and free will—where the universe may guide us toward love, but our choices shape its course. Whether love is predestined or created, one truth remains: it is one of life's greatest journeys, filled with wonder, discovery, and the profound power of human connection.

Soulmates and Serendipity: Are We Meant to Be?

The idea of soulmates has long been a topic of fascination, inspiring poetry, literature, and deep philosophical debates. Many believe that somewhere in the world, there exists one perfect person destined to complete them, as if love is predetermined by fate. The concept of soulmates suggests that two people are cosmically connected, drawn together by forces beyond their control. Serendipitous encounters, unexpected reunions, and uncanny similarities between partners often make people wonder if love is truly meant to be. These moments of fate make relationships feel extraordinary, as if the universe conspired to bring two hearts together at precisely the right time.

Serendipity plays a significant role in how people perceive love and destiny. Stories of lovers meeting by chance, crossing paths repeatedly, or finding each other in the most unexpected circumstances give the impression that some connections are simply meant to happen. Many people can recall moments in their own lives when they met someone and felt an immediate, unexplainable bond, as if they had known each other before. These experiences often reinforce the belief that some relationships are not mere coincidences but rather a part of a grand design. Love, in this sense, feels magical—

something beyond logic, beyond planning, beyond mere human decisions.

Yet, as romantic as the idea of soulmates may be, love is also a choice. Even the strongest connections require effort, patience, and commitment to flourish. A relationship that feels destined will not last without nurturing, communication, and shared growth. Fate may bring two people together, but it is their willingness to work through challenges that determines whether the love will stand the test of time. While some believe in the idea of a single, predestined soulmate, others argue that love is not about finding someone perfect, but about choosing to build something meaningful with the right person. Love evolves, shaped by decisions and experiences, making it more than just an act of destiny.

Some people find deep, lasting love multiple times in their lives, suggesting that the notion of one exclusive soulmate may be limiting. Relationships are complex, and what feels like destiny at one stage of life may transform into a different path later on. Rather than searching for a predetermined soulmate, many people create their own fate by embracing the relationships that bring them joy, challenge them to grow, and align with their values. Love may not always arrive in the form expected, but it often finds a way when the heart is open to it.

Perhaps love is a delicate balance between fate and free will. There may be moments that feel orchestrated by the universe, but it is the choices made within a relationship that determine its depth and longevity. Whether love is written in the stars or shaped by human effort, it remains one of life's greatest mysteries—an experience that continues to evolve, surprise, and redefine itself with every new encounter. Soulmates may exist, but perhaps they are not found; they are created, built through shared moments, trust, and a deep, intentional commitment to love.

Love, Free Will, and the Choices We Make

Love is often seen as a force of destiny, something that happens to us rather than something we actively control. Many people believe in the idea that love is written in the stars, that two people are meant to be together no matter what. However, love is not solely dictated by fate; it is also shaped by free will and the choices we make every day. While serendipity may play a role in bringing people together, it is the conscious decisions within a relationship that determine its strength, longevity, and meaning. Love is not just about finding the right person—it is about choosing to nurture, sustain, and grow with them through all of life's changes.

The notion of free will in love emphasizes the power of choice. From the moment two people meet, their relationship is built on a series of decisions—choosing to open up, to trust, to commit, and to invest time and energy into one another. Love is not simply about the initial spark of attraction or the magic of a "meant-to-be" connection; it is about the conscious effort put into maintaining that connection. Relationships do not succeed by accident. They thrive when two individuals choose to communicate openly, respect one another, and actively work toward a shared future. The idea that love is solely an uncontrollable force can sometimes lead to complacency, whereas recognizing the role of free will empowers people to take responsibility for their relationships.

At the same time, love is not always predictable. Despite best intentions and mutual effort, some relationships may not last. Free will means that people change, grow apart, or face challenges that make continuing a relationship difficult. The choices we make in love are not just about staying together; sometimes, they involve letting go when necessary. Love is about learning when to fight for a connection and when to accept that two paths are no longer aligned. The beauty of free will in love is that it allows people to make decisions based on what is best for their happiness and well-being rather than being bound by the idea of fate alone.

Free will also means that love is not limited to just one person or one experience. While some believe in the concept of a single soulmate, life often presents multiple opportunities for deep, meaningful love. People grow and evolve, and with each stage of life, new connections may emerge. The ability to love again after heartbreak, loss, or change is a testament to the resilience of the human heart. Love is not a one-time event dictated by destiny—it is a continuous journey influenced by the choices we make.

Ultimately, love is a balance between fate and free will. While chance may bring two people together, it is their choices that determine whether they stay together. Love is about choosing to show up, to care, to be kind, and to grow alongside another person. In the end, the power of love lies not in destiny alone, but in the decisions that shape its course, making it one of life's most beautiful and transformative experiences.

Conclusion

Love is one of the most powerful and transformative forces in the human experience. It manifests in countless forms—romantic, platonic, familial, and self-love—each contributing to the richness of life. Love has the power to heal wounds, strengthen bonds, inspire change, and create a sense of belonging that transcends time and space. Through the journey of understanding love, from its passionate beginnings to its enduring presence, we come to realize that love is not just about grand gestures or fleeting emotions; it is about the choices we make, the commitment we uphold, and the connections we nurture.

Throughout history, love has been perceived as both an uncontrollable force of fate and a conscious decision. While some believe that love is written in the stars, predetermined by destiny, others recognize the role of free will in shaping relationships. Love may begin with a serendipitous encounter or an inexplicable bond, but it thrives through effort, understanding, and emotional investment. It is not just about finding someone special—it is about choosing to build something meaningful every day. Relationships, whether romantic or otherwise, require patience, kindness, and the ability to grow alongside one another.

In a world increasingly dominated by technology and digital interactions, maintaining genuine emotional intimacy has become more challenging yet more essential than ever. Love must be actively cultivated, not just through words, but through actions that reaffirm care, trust, and respect. It requires presence—both physical and emotional—where partners, friends, and family members feel valued and heard. Love is not about perfection but about the willingness to navigate imperfections together, embracing both the joys and challenges that come with deep connections.

Self-love is just as vital as the love we give to others. Before we can fully love another, we must first understand and accept ourselves. Self-love is not selfish; it is the foundation upon which all other relationships are built. By prioritizing self-care, setting boundaries, and practicing self-compassion, we cultivate an inner strength that allows us to love others more fully. Love is not meant to complete us; rather, it should enhance who we already are. When we recognize our own worth, we attract relationships that are rooted in mutual respect and appreciation.

As we reflect on the journey of love, it becomes clear that love is not just about romance or passion—it is about connection, growth, and the legacy we leave behind. Love is found in the small, everyday moments: a comforting hug, a kind word, an act of selflessness, or the unwavering support of a friend. The way we love—through patience, understanding, and kindness—shapes not only our relationships but also the world around us. Love is not confined to a single moment or a single relationship; it is an ongoing journey that continues to evolve throughout our lives.

In the end, love is both a gift and a responsibility. It is something we receive, but also something we give. It is an ever-expanding force that, when nurtured, grows beyond ourselves and into the hearts of others. Whether guided by fate, free will, or a combination of both, love remains the most profound and enduring aspect of human existence. It is through love that we find meaning, and through love that we leave a lasting impact on the world.

www.ingramcontent.com/pod-product-compliance
Lightning Source LLC
LaVergne TN
LVHW061527070526
838199LV00009B/394